The Wisdom of Cerridwen: Transforming Her Cosmic Brew

Girl God Books

Edited by Emma Clark
Pat Daly, and Trista Hendren

Preface by H. Byron Ballard

Cover Art by Reti Toriella

ISBN: 978-82-93725-57-2

www.thegirlgod.com

The views expressed in this anthology are solely those of the author and do not necessarily reflect the views of the publisher.

None of the information presented in this book is meant to replace the advice of a medical, health, legal and/or any other professional or service. How you choose to act on the words and content is of your own determination and free will.

www.thegirlgod.com

Girl God Books

Warrior Queen: Answering the Call of The Morrigan

A powerful anthology about the Irish Celtic Goddess. Each contributor brings The Morrigan to life with unique stories that invite readers to partake and inspire them to pen their own. Included are essays, poems, stories, chants, rituals, and art from dozens of story-tellers and artists from around the world, illustrating and recounting the many ways this powerful Goddess of war, death, and prophecy has changed their lives.

Re-Membering with Goddess: Healing the Patriarchal Perpetuation of Trauma is an anthology of women's experiences of trauma—trauma as a result of patriarchy; trauma perpetuated by patriarchy; and how through personal healing of trauma the Goddess is re-membered, re-embodied and resurrected. As repeating loops of trauma restriction release—in the mind, body and nervous system—Goddess is re-embodied and rises... and the patriarchy falls.

The Crone Initiation: Women Speak on the Menopause Journey

The Crone Initiation is an anthology of women's experiences of perimenopause and menopause, and the part Goddess plays in this journey. Crone's presence in the breakdowns and breakthroughs, the disintegration and rebuilding, is expressed through words and art. Meaning is reclaimed and the power of the Elder restored.

Women's Sovereignty and Body Autonomy Beyond Roe v. Wade addresses the concerns and opinions of women from around the planet. Through art and poetry, prose and personal accounts, this shared atrocity that continues to be forced on women is brought into a new light with a rebel resolve that screams "NO MORE"!

Re-visioning Medusa: from Monster to Divine Wisdom

A remarkable collection of essays, poems, and art by scholars who have researched Her, artists who have envisioned Her, and women who have known Her in their personal story. All have spoken with Her and share something of their communion in this anthology.

Inanna's Ascent: Reclaiming Female Power

Inanna's Ascent examines how females can rise from the underworld and reclaim their power, sovereignly expressed through poetry, prose and visual art. All contributors are extraordinary women in their own right, who have been through some difficult life lessons—and are brave enough to share their stories.

Just as I Am: Hymns Affirming the Divine Female

What is a Hermnal? It's the collective sigh of our ancestral Grandmothers. It's a means of drawing us closer together as Sisters. It is a compilation of songs that affirm our Sacredness, apart from Man, and assures us that we are Sovereign Beings and Creatrixes, too. And it is our Love Gift of Gratitude to Mama.

In Defiance of Oppression – The Legacy of Boudicca

An anthology that encapsulates the Spirit of the defiant warrior in a modern apathetic age. No longer will the voices of our sisters go unheard, as the ancient Goddesses return to the battlements, calling to ignite the spark within each and every one of us—to defy oppression wherever we find it, and stand together in solidarity.

Original Resistance: Reclaiming Lilith, Reclaiming Ourselves

As women across the globe rise up against the patriarchy, Lilith stands beside them, misogyny's original challenger. This anthology—a chorus of voices hitting chords of defiance, liberation, anger and joy—reclaims the goodness of women bold enough to hold tight to their essence.

Willendorf's Legacy: The Sacred Body

Travel through time and discover a world where the fullness of women was both admired and deified. Reclaim your beautiful Goddess body through the rich pages of this powerful collection of art, poetry and essays celebrating our divine inheritance as daughters of Willendorf.

Complete list of Girl God publications at www.thegirlgod.com

"To respell the world means to redefine the root of our being. It means to redefine us and therefore change us by returning us to our original consciousness of magical-evolutionary processes. This consciousness is within us, in our biology and in our dreams... When we are aware of it, it works for us, as the energy of destiny.

And it is powerful."

-Monica Sjöö and Barbara Mor, *The Great Cosmic Mother*

In Remembrance of our Beautiful Sister and Priestess of Cerridwen, Kate Greenwood.

(7th December 1972 – 23rd December 2024)

Thank you for all your wisdom and green magick.

May you dance with the trees in Annwfn.

Photo of Kate by Sadie Laurenti Whitley.

Table of Contents

Foreword

H. Byron Ballard

Cerridwen, ancient Queen,
Dark Mother, take us in.
Cerridwen, ancient Queen,
Let us be reborn.
—a Reclaiming chant

Open these pages and relish the words of this divine Mother, this wild Sister, this trickster and keeper of the Cauldron of Eternity! Spend time with Her. Learn Her sacred ways, Her stories, Her lore.

I learned the chant above at the Glastonbury Goddess Conference where I taught several years ago. I often use it in both my private meditations and in public rituals. It is simple but direct, quite unlike the Goddess it honors. I learned how to pronounce Her name from a Welsh-speaking colleague who gave it a rolling "r" and an emphasis on the second syllable. Keh-RRRHID-wen. Try it. So delicious to say.

The first tale I read about Her was the shape-shifting riddle game of the Goddess and Gwion Bach, who was to be reborn as the legendary Welsh poet, Taliesin. She set the boy to stir a powerful brew that would grant Her son wisdom to compensate for his ugly appearance. But the hot potion splashed onto the boy's thumb and he stuck it in his mouth, thus gaining what was meant for Cerridwen's son. The Goddess chased the boy who kept changing his shape. She did the same and the chase ended with Gwion Bach transforming into a grain of wheat and She changing into a hen that swallowed him up. But because the boy had tasted the magical brew, the Goddess became pregnant and birthed Taliesin.

But my favorite story by far is the one I tell every Samhain and use as an example of the Otherworld in many Pagan groups. It goes like this:

When we make the transition from matter to spirit, our souls go into the West, to a place called the Summerlands, the Applelands or sometimes Tir Nan Og, the Land of Youth. There are beautiful green fields there with streams of fresh and sweet water. The Gods and the Ancestors abide there, amongst vast apple orchards. On each tree, there is every stage of an apple's life—bud to blossom, green apple to ripe one, even rotting apples are supported by each tree's branches.

When our souls arrive in this place, we rest and walk with the Divines and the Ancestors, refreshing ourselves by drinking the sweet water and learning from our kindred who have already made the journey.

When we are ready, we review our lives and discuss them to gain understanding of why we did what we did and to ponder some wisdom. When we are ready, we make the decision to stay in this peaceful place and become on Ancestor or to return for another try at human life.

If the choice is to return, the essence of our being returns to the great cauldron of Cerridwen where it joins the remnants of the souls of our whole tribe in a sort of spirit stew. And when a new baby is born, the great Goddess scoops out just enough soul for that particular baby. On the baby's first cry, Cerridwen pours in the perfect amount of that soul stew for this new human.

No Hell, no punishment, only apples, sweet water and the people we came from. Only understanding and wisdom, and a decision based on both. Then a reunion with the essence of us all before we start the whole process again. All in the hands of this magnificent Being, this shape-shifting Mother who tenderly holds our souls until we are ready for rebirth.

Let these words and artwork guide you to Her, in all Her forms and guises. Prepare yourself for a many-faceted jewel with beauty and wisdom to share with Her people. And know that you are Her people.

*Swynwraig, Healer and Witch**

Reti Toriella

* Swynwraig: a lady who knows her magic and the healing power of plants.

The Wisdom of Cerridwen

Emma Clark

What does it take to make a spell? A wisdom brew? It always starts with the woman. With the Goddess. It starts with Her breath, Her incantation, Her will. It is a process of co-creation between Her own self and that which She adds to Her cauldron. She is a WITCH – a Woman In Total Control of Herself (as the apron which hangs in my kitchen proudly proclaims). Cerridwen is the archetypal Witch Goddess and yet, for centuries, She has not been in charge of Her own narrative. Others, usually men, have written Her story down in manuscripts within the Welsh tradition and it is important to remember that while they may have been looking back on older beliefs, they were doing this through a Christian lens and they come with their own agendas and biases.

Two 16th century manuscripts tell the story of Cerridwen, namely Elis Gruffudd's *Chronicle of the History of the World* (National Library of Wales, MS 5276D) and John Jones of Gellilyfdy's Peniarth MS 111 (National Library of Wales). The Celtic scholar, Kristoffer Hughes, has highlighted the differing connection of both writers to the tale. While Elis Gruffudd feels 'no great passion and simply copies the tale from a subsequently vanished text and whatever oral sources were available to him' (Hughes, 2019, p. 27), John Jones seems to appreciate the mystery of Cerridwen's story and may have taken his inspiration from the oral tradition (Hughes, 2019, p. 28). The late 16th century bard, Llewellyn Siôn also records a version and this fragment can, like the others, be found in the National Library of Wales (NLW 13075b).

Cerridwen is also present in poetry attributed to the famous bard, Taliesin. In 'Taliesin's Song of his Origins' he recounts his memories:

> Firstly I was formed in the shape of a handsome man,
> In the hall of Cerridwen in order to be refined.

Although small and modest in my behaviour,
I was great in her lofty sanctuary.

While I was held prisoner, sweet inspiration educated me
And laws were imparted me in a speech which had no words;
But I had to flee the angry terrible hag
Whose outcry was terrifying.

(translated from the Welsh by Caitlín and John Matthews, 2002, p. 281)

The hall of Cerridwen is Her womb, and Her outcry can be interpreted as the cries of Her labour as She births Taliesin (Matthews, 2002, p. 282). In 'Primary Chief Bard', Taliesin again mentions that:

I was nine full months
In the womb of the hag Cerridwen
Before that I was Gwion,
But now I am Taliesin.

In 'The Chair of Cerridwen' also from the Book of Taliesin, Taliesin may or may not be acting as a mouthpiece for Cerridwen but either way, the words (even in translation) are powerful and magically incantatory:

This is my chair, my cauldron, and these are my rules,
My perfect language is a consistent chair,
In the court of Don, I am the knowledgeable one,
...
My chair is kept, it is here,
And it will be maintained in Europe...

(translated from the Welsh by Kristoffer Hughes, 2021, pp. 73-74)

Kristoffer Hughes makes a compelling case for the voice in the poem being the narrative spirit, 'the element of the bard that swims within the currents of Awen.' (Hughes, 2021, p. 74). Down the centuries, Cerridwen has been worshipped and derided by the Bards in the same way that the Muse has been treated by the Romantic poets. It is all good until the Goddess withdraws Her inspiration and then Her beauty is forgotten, and She is described as a hag or a witch.

In recent years, there have been steps taken to allow Cerridwen and Her story to breathe in the air of a new time. She no longer needs to be conveniently packaged for a Christian readership and we can now read between the previously rigid lines of manuscript and let the inspiration of the tale take us to the timeless place of orality. Bee Helygen, a teacher and Priestess of Cerridwen, describes those who are inspired by Cerridwen today, and how a thread of remembrance touches them at Cerridwen's Lake Bala.

> Suddenly each sister takes the hand of the woman standing next to her, reaching out, remembering that they have done this many eons ago, they confidently step deeper into the waters...
> (Helygen and Clark, 2023, p.14)

Perhaps this is the only authentic way to fully understand any Goddess. The manuscripts can only take us so far. And then we must carry on along the road using our own means of intuition, imagination and vision. Only then will Cerridwen begin to reveal to us the wisdom in the depths of Her cauldron.

Cerridwen is not only a Mother Goddess. She is also a Goddess of Matrescence. Aurélie Athan, a clinical psychologist specialising in maternal and reproductive health, describes Matrescence as a spiritual awakening, an initiation that does not end and, instead, keeps unfolding (Athan and Miller, 2013, p. 220). There are many parallels with this idea and the story of Cerridwen. She embodies the traits of a fierce but loving Mother Goddess, but perhaps more importantly, we see Her motherhood journey unfolding within Her own story. The catalyst for the making of Her wisdom brew is Her own son, Morfran. She learns so much about Herself as She moves through the initiation of Matrescence. Can a Goddess also be an initiate? Cerridwen shows us that this is a possibility, and thus, Her story is a gentle reminder to all women to give ourselves permission to learn, to make mistakes (the brew is perhaps not the best answer for Her son), to rest (as She does when the brew is almost complete), to let go of old ideas and patterns (as She does when She lets go of Her own plan and embraces Taliesin) and, crucially for ourselves and the planet, there is also the seed of permission to start a-new.

I am conscious that I came to Cerridwen as my own journey into motherhood deepened. I am absolutely certain that motherhood is not the only access point to this Goddess. She inspires me in many ways; every time I create, write and sing. Whenever I feel the flow of Awen, I feel Cerridwen's influence, but it is Cerridwen's motherhood journey which reaches my softest, most vulnerable places and allows me to breathe into those places – my breath and Her breath combined.

I never expected motherhood to change me completely, but it did. Perhaps that is the true meaning of initiation. Like a greyhound, otter and hawk, I chased the idea of being a mother through my early years of womanhood and on into my thirties. I had an inclination of what it would be like, but the reality was all-encompassing and I revelled in this newfound identity. Things which had niggled and worried me before – the everyday 'stuff of life' – paled into insignificance when I looked at my daughter. I want to be clear here that not every woman has to become a mother to feel like this. In fact, there is a little part of me which feels embarrassed that it was motherhood which caused me to 'wake up'. Others may find their awakening comes in other forms and by ways of other catalysts. But I had walked the path of the scholar for many years, and I think that perhaps the world of academia had resulted in an over-reliance on my intellect and less emphasis on the corporeal. When Cerridwen created Her wisdom-brew, She consulted the book of the Pheryllt, the ancient magicians and keepers of magic and science who lived in the mountains of Eryri. However, book learning was not enough, and I found this on a personal level too. Intellect and emotion came together and simmered in my womb-cauldron brew. Motherhood made me more aware of my own body and the land on which I placed my feet. Cerridwen had to go out onto the land at different times of the day and night and in the different seasons to gather the plants that were needed for the brew. The wisdom-brew was, partly, an embodiment of Cerridwen's dedication to magic and motherhood. She had to put Her own energy into it. She had to slow down and look for what She needed, watch the turning seasons and develop patience. I could sympathize with that slowness of living. As the mother of a young child, my world shrunk rather gloriously in the beginning! I walked with the pram and then the buggy along the same paths each day. I noticed the plants growing through the cracks in the pavement (those much derided 'weeds', which I came to love as companions and which I now know are actually our native allies) and I found joy in the apps on my phone which helped me to identify the plants which I did not know as I took long walks in nature, as my daughter slept with the motion of the walk.

But with this newfound mindfulness, also came something else. The fierce protective rage of a mother's love, not just for my own daughter but for all children. It poured through me and affected my decisions and my stance on everything. Motherhood simultaneously softened and strengthened me. The anger I feel when I read local and international news of atrocities against mothers and children is like a cauldron boiling over. For me, Cerridwen is a very 'human' Goddess, because Her attempt to make things easier for Her son is such a relatable response. Many mothers will understand the feeling of hoping their child can fit in and be accepted in the world, even while believing in the importance of their child's own identity and sense of self. Every inner and outer battle I have fought on behalf of my now school age daughter, every dark night of the soul I have experienced as I worry for her present and future life, has been experienced with Cerridwen in my heart. Cerridwen made the choice to do something for Morfran (even if it was not the 'right' choice in the long run). It has been said that Cerridwen achieved apotheosis at this time – that the making of the brew, the subsequent initiatory chase of Gwion Bach, the birthing of Taliesin and the realisation that Taliesin was not hers to keep but should instead be given to the world which so badly needed his wisdom and inspirational poetry, was actually Her own initiation. Even Goddesses are transformed in the cauldron. This is the seed of wisdom for me in the story. For I know in my bones that while I may teach my daughter about the world, she is constantly teaching and initiating me as we journey together, just as Cerridwen's own children initiated Her into deeper wisdom. We have to actually live our lives, brew the potion, make the spell, birth the creation, to fully understand it.

I find Cerridwen in the dark woods of the witch. I find Her in my kitchen as I bring the pot to the boil, I find Her in the bird's flight above me, and the rustle of quick-footed animals in the undergrowth on a misty morning. She is the magic Matriarch of the Mysteries, the Faery Queen of the Otherworld, the whisper of poetry and song as it forms in the air around me. She touches my radiant brow, and I taste a little of the wisdom, of all that is possible in our world, but I know that I need to chase it across earth, sea and sky if I am to understand more. She is the raging mother, the protective mother, the wronged mother and all of the facets of motherhood in between. She meets me at the centre of the labyrinth as I wind my way in and out of life's lessons. I know Her in the autumn, as the descent into the earth begins. She is waiting in the roundhouse of the Bards in the darkest of winter nights, in the scent of snow and fir. She is the crackle of the regenerative spring fire and the heat haze of summer when everything shimmers and the possibilities seem endless. She is in my grandmother's ladle, stirring the porridge pot and She is in my mother's concerned voice, searching and hoping that I am safe. And She is in every creation from every woman in this book, every woman who has had the courage to hear Her call and become a conduit of the Awen.

References

Primary Sources:
NLW MS 5276D. *Chronicle of the History of the World.* Elis Gruffudd. Circa 1552.

NLW 13075b. Rhyddiaith. Llywelyn Siôn and 'Iolo Morganwg'. Peniarth Manuscript 111. Hanes Taliesin. John Jones. 1607.

Athan, Aurelie and Miller, Lisa. (2013). 'Motherhood as Opportunity to Learn Spiritual Values: Experiences and Insights of New Mothers.' *Journal of Prenatal and Perinatal Psychology and Health* 27. 220-253.

Helygen, Bee and Clark, Emma (eds.) (2023). *In Her Dark Bright Spirit: A Journey with the Goddess Cerridwen* (Glastonbury: Blue Cedar).

Hughes, Kristoffer. (2019). *From the Cauldron Born: Exploring the Magic of Welsh Legend and Lore* (Minesota: Llewellyn Publications).

Hughes, Kristoffer. (2021). *Cerridwen: Celtic Goddess of Inspiration* (Minesota: Llewellyn Publications).

Matthews, John and Caitlín. (2002). *Taliesin: The Last Celtic Shaman*. (Vermont: Inner Traditions).

Wheat Seed Lady

Reti Toriella

A Note About this Anthology

Trista Hendren

The Wisdom of Cerridwen contains a variety of writing styles from people around the world. Various forms of English are included in this anthology and we chose to keep spellings of the writers' place of origin to honor/honour everyone's unique voice.

It was the expressed intent of the editors to not police standards of citation, transliteration and formatting. Contributors have determined which citation style, italicization policy and transliteration system to adopt in their pieces. The resulting diversity reflects the diversity of academic fields, genres and personal expressions represented by the authors. [1]

When Emma Clark came to me about publishing several books on Cerridwen, I did not know much about Her. Years prior, I had come across a small Cerridwen plaque by Maxine Miller on Etsy that I fell in love with. I purchased it and hung it at my entryway.

I knew nothing about Cerridwen when I bought the artwork, but She spoke to me. I knew after talking to Emma that we had to put out these books. She had been waiting patiently for me at my door for many years.

As Jhenah Telyndru discusses at length in a later chapter, there are various spellings and pronunciations of Her name. My dear sister Susan Morgaine had to teach me how to pronounce Cerridwen, so I was happy when Village Witch Byron Ballard included that in her Preface. It is endlessly sad to me how much is suppressed from our knowing. Mary Daly wrote long ago that, "Women have had the

---

[1] This paragraph is borrowed and adapted with love from *A Jihad for Justice: Honoring the Work and Life of Amina Wadud*. Edited by Kecia Ali, Juliane Hammer and Laury Silvers.

power of naming stolen from us." [2] The quest for our own naming, and our own language, is never-ending, and each of us attempts it differently.

People often get caught up on whether we say Divine Female or Divine Feminine. Personally, I try to just listen to what the speaker is trying to say. The fact remains that few of us were privileged with a woman-affirming education—and we all have a lot of time to make up for. Let's all be gentle with each other through that process.

If you find that a particular writing doesn't sit well with you, please feel free to use the Al-Anon suggestion: "Take what you like, leave the rest!" That said, if there aren't at least several pieces that challenge you, we have not done our job here.

We are living in violently unsettling times. It is more important than ever to take good care of ourselves, our families, and our communities. Cerridwen's medicine is vital; Her wisdom irreplaceable. As Danielle Dulsky wrote:

> "How heavy the healer's hands become in these times. Our healer ancestors served their small circles, their local communities, their tribes. Their role was paramount to a village and to a land. They spoke the language of the mountains and the sea. They knew every plant that grew near their homes, and they tended these medicines with great care, knowing precisely what ailments afflicted their people and what remedies the land spirits could offer. What has become of the healer in these times, when we can scroll through so many sicknesses on our small screens in a matter of moments? Just as these times warrant new stories and

---

[2] Daly, Mary. *Gyn/Ecology: The Metaethics of Radical Feminism*. Beacon Press, 1990.

> new ways of being, our rapidly shifting world is ravenous for radical healing." [3]

It is time to come back into our innate, sacred wisdom—and take back the world that was stolen from us. Merely "surviving" under Capitalist Patriarchy is a brutality that we were never meant to endure.

So, prepare your cauldron! It is time to rise with the Awen of Cerridwen.

---

[3] Dulsky, Danielle. *The Holy Wild Grimoire: A Heathen Handbook of Magick, Spells, and Verses*. New World Library; September 13, 2022.

The Crone

Kat Shaw

Cerridwen Invocation

Rebekah Myers

Cerridwen,
from your sacred Cauldron,
we are transformed.
Keeper of Knowledge;
Shape-Shifter;
Mother;
Prophetess,
give us the "Awen,"
the "Grace of your Inspiration."
Give us your energy,
your tenacity;
give us your mystic power.
May all our right desires
be brought to fullness!
All Hail, Cerridwen!

Goddess Ceridwen – Changing this World Begins with Our Own Personal Transformation

Dorothy Collin

The wild and dramatically beautiful Welsh landscape, with its lush green valleys and rolling mountains, is home to the Goddess Ceridwen, muse through the ages, Goddess of rebirth and transformation, poetic inspiration in a land with a long and rich history of poets and bards.

It was through the power of Ceridwen's cauldron that great knowledge and inspiration (Awen) could be gained, essential for the transformation and empowerment of individuals. Ceridwen wished to give these great gifts to her beloved son Morfran, whom the world in its shallow and vain appraisal of humans, saw as ugly, dark and repugnant, especially in contrast with his sister Creirwy, who was fair, beautiful and good. This disturbing and ever present idea that dark is evil and fair is good.

Ceridwen's love for her son inspired her to try and help him thrive in such a hard, unkind world but her plans were accidentally thwarted when her young servant, Gwion Bach, drank the first three drops of the potion meant for Morfran and so gained the great knowledge and inspiration that should have been his. Gwion fled, fearing Ceridwen's wrath and thus ensued a great chase through the land, through the changing of seasons and the shapeshifting of both Gwion and Ceridwen. Each of his transformations was surpassed by Ceridwen, her greyhound to his hare, her otter to his fish, her hawk to his small bird and finally her shapeshifting into a hen to eat his ear of corn.

Her rebirth of Gwion months later transformed him into the great poet Taliesin and there was in fact a historical poet of that name in the sixth century. One of the few poems that can be possibly attributed to him is the *Battle of Goddeu* where he begins by speaking of all the profusion of shapes he has been, before he became his present everlasting form.

The absence of the Goddess is so keenly felt in our world today and everything that Ceridwen wanted to give to her son is everything that we should wish for ourselves, for our children and for the children of the world in their quest for acceptance, inspiration, and knowledge.

The gift of rebirth; to seek out a new life within our present one, to birth ourselves into the shape and form we would truly wish to be, one that is faithful to who we are within and not what the world would have us be, one that is deeply connected to all around us and not divided and estranged from where we all once began.

The gift of transformation; to change, to grow, to develop, to never stop learning, adapting, empowering ourselves and others, secure in the understanding that life is not a stagnant, stunted pool devoid of ebb and flow, resistant to new ideas, feelings and experiences, but in fact this life is an ever rushing torrent of colours and vibrant emotions just waiting for each of us to embrace all that we are and all that everyone else around us is too.

The gift of knowledge; for what is more important for the human mind than to continuously learn and grow in a world so full of wisdom that we would need a hundred lifetimes to even begin to tap the surface?

At no time in history has there been a greater need for the transformative powers of Ceridwen and the inspiration and knowledge that can be found deep inside her cauldron. The wonder and beauty of Awen, the need for all of us to use our words to create new meaning, new visions of who we want to be and the type of world we want to see built around us. The horror and hatred which has governed us all for far too long must die and from its ashes we must rebirth this world with all the love and wisdom of the Goddess to protect everyone.

There is so much violent death in the world right now that surely a transformation is at hand, surely it is time for our communal awakening, surely, we need to establish a greater wisdom within us and our communities. It starts within each of us, a rebirth into a life filled anew with greater wisdom, connections and a sense of transformative power. An awakening from a hideous slumber of darkness inside an odious existence of suffering and destruction into a life filled with the energy of enlightenment and knowledge and all the power that such a transformation can bring to us and those around us.

So, allow yourself to feel the power of Ceridwen. She will whisper to you in the gentle breeze as it rushes over the land or you may see her in the wild animals as they briefly catch you in their sight. When you feel her presence, you will know that your time of regeneration is near at hand, if you are just brave enough to grasp it.

Biddy Early

Andrea Redmond

Embodied Mentorship with the Goddess Cerridwen

Kay Louise Aldred

Cerridwen is the Welsh Goddess of inspiration (Awen), transformation, and rebirth. She is one face of the Dark Goddess, often depicted as a 'hag' and considered to be the Goddess of the moon, magic, and the cauldron. She was a mystic, witch, and sorceress, and is a perfect mentor for the season of Samhain.

This Goddess offers us many gifts – predominantly the cauldron of abundance and the blessing of Awen, which is the energy of creative inspiration, prophecy, and wisdom. The main legend about her cauldron involves her son Afagddu and servant boy Gwion. Cerridwen wanted her son to be a seer and set about creating a magical potion to ensure this within her cauldron. This brew needed to be stirred for a year and a day, so she instructed Gwion to do this but to not drink any of it himself. One day the potion bubbled vigorously, and three drops splattered onto Gwion's hand. He licked them and received potent wisdom and power.

The Legend continues with Cerridwen furiously chasing Gwion. During the chase, both continuously shapeshift and metamorphosise. The chase is one of transformation and ends in Gwion being eaten in the form of a grain when she is a hen. The story reader assumes this is the death of the boy but in her belly, he is regenerated and reborn as an inspired, Awen-fuelled poet.

Her body, as is ours, is the vehicle for change. We can process the underworld, and all emotions, including anger and fear, and change our DNA and ancestral patterns through a metamorphic staged journey. Cerridwen is aware of the profound impact of cauldron, spells, and elixirs, and teaches us to take our magic and magical tools very seriously. From her we activate our sight, our third eye.

Extract from *Mentorship with Goddess: Growing Sacred Womanhood;* Girl God Books, 2022.

Cauldron of Cerridwen

Rebekah Myers

The Welsh Goddess, Cerridwen, as Mother, Matriarch, and Crone bestows upon us vital gifts of transformation, adaptability, tenacity, death/renewal, knowledge, clarity, and inspiration of all kinds.

Cerridwen is a shape-shifting moon goddess. Sacred to her are the white sow and the hen. Her trees are the hazel and apple, and her magical herb brewing includes acorns, sow's thistle, vervain, hellebore and more. Poetry and writing are sacred to Cerridwen, and Welsh bards were called "the sons of Cerridwen," receiving their initiation directly from her. The three potent drops from her Cauldron are the "Awen," or "The Grace of Inspiration."

Cerridwen teaches us that we can adapt and change to make the most of whatever situation we find ourselves in; to transform challenges into strengths.

From her we learn the "change of plans" so essential to the survivor. In the Womb of her Cauldron, we die and are reborn, shining with knowledge, poetry, strength, magic, and the power to bring our desires to fullness.

Hail to Cerridwen!
Awen!

- How might you write your own story?
- How might you create a "Plan B?"
- How might you seek and share inspiration?

Cerridwen – Lady of the Cauldron

Lisbeth Cheever-Gessaman

Ceridwen - Divine Muse and Mother of Awen

Jhenah Telyndru

Muse and Mother. Shapeshifter and change maker. Goddess and witch.

It is as difficult to pin Ceridwen down to any one role, or to fully understand the complexities of her fundamental nature, as it is to uncover the meaning of her very name. Because there weren't yet uniform spellings of the Welsh language when the first vernacular poems and stories were being written down in the early medieval period, many versions of Ceridwen's name appear in early Welsh literature — shifting and changing over time before being standardized in Modern Welsh as Ceridwen or Cerridwen. On the surface, this may not seem like much of an issue, but it does complicate tracing the etymology of her name — depriving us of information that could be helpful to our understanding of her cultural significance.

But we are not without information, and while the various potential meanings of her name derived from the etymologies based on the myriad spellings of her name are suggestive rather than definitive, perhaps this is fitting for a shapeshifting figure who wields the powerful essence of creation.

Celticist and Welsh Scholar Marged Haycock postulates the following: [4]

1. Cwrr-rhid-ben - an angular or crooked woman, or woman with angular embrace
2. Cryt-ben - a fevered woman
3. Creit-fen - a passionate or inflamed woman
4. Credid-fen - a woman that one as a belief or faith in

---

[4] Marged Haycock, *Legendary Poems from the Book of Taliesin*, 2nd ed. (Aberystwyth: Centre for Medieval Studies, 2015), 320.

While Mary Jones offers these potential meanings for her name: [5]

> 1. Ceritwen > *cerid-* and *-wen* - "loved and fair"
> 2. Ceritwen > *cyrrid* + *ben*: *cyrrid* ‹*cwrr* "hooked, crooked" cf. Ir. *corrán* :hook, sickle; *ben* < *benyw* "woman": "crooked [back?] woman"
> 3. Ceritwen › *cyrrid* + *gwen*: "crooked white one"

Other scholars have forwarded the following possibilities:

> 1. Holy Song - "cerdd" - song, poetry, "wen" - white, shining, holy
> 2. Crooked Woman or Bent White One - "cyrrid + ben" (Ir)- hooked or crooked + woman
> 3. Shining Beloved One/Fair and Loved - from "cariad" - love [6]

And finally, in his excellent book *Cerridwen: Celtic Goddess of Inspiration*, Kristoffer Hughes compiles the various possibilities into a summary meaning for Cerridwen as "a blessed, holy woman of angular bending magic." [7]

The allusion to a "bent white one" and the connection to the word for sickle in Irish can certainly conjure up the image of an old woman, bent over as she reaps in the harvest or gathers healing herbs from the countryside. However, it is possible this may allude to Ceridwen having a lunar connection, meant to describe the crescent moon instead. As we may never be sure of the exact meaning of Ceridwen's name, perhaps those who are or seek to be in devotional relationship with her can determine for themselves which one best reflects the nature of the Goddess as they have

---

[5] "Cerridwen", *Mary Jones: Celtic Encyclopedia*. https://www.maryjones.us/jce/cerridwen.html [accessed: 16 April 2025].

[6] Rachel Bromwich, *Trioedd Ynys Prydein: The Welsh Triads* (Cardiff: University of Wales Press, 2006), 312.

[7] Kristoffer Hughes, *Cerridwen: Celtic Goddess of Inspiration* (Woodbury, MN: Llewellyn Worldwide, 2019), 91.

come to know her. Fortunately, name etymology is not our only source of information about Ceridwen.

Mam Yr Awen

In Welsh bardic tradition, the figure of Ceridwen looms large as the Mother of Bards, serving as their primary Muse. Her cauldron is extolled as the source of the Awen — the breath of divine inspiration that bestows poetry and prophecy — and it is Ceridwen herself who determines who is worthy of Awen's blessings. She is depicted as an exacting judge; giver of the rules of rhyme and meter of poetic song, Ceridwen demands excellence from the bards who would seek the bounty of her cauldron.

Like other Celtic cultures, the Welsh and their Brythonic predecessors practiced oral tradition, choosing to transmit their cultural history, lineages of the nobility, and ancient wisdom tales in orality rather than committing them to writing. Because of this, the formally trained bards of Wales played an important cultural role that is believed to have originated in the Iron Age pre-Christian period, extending through the sub-Roman era and the middle ages, and their influence remains present into the modern day. Even after some of their works began to be written down in the medieval period, they remained important figures in the courts of Welsh nobility.

Bards were tasked with reciting histories and trancing lineages, performing native stories and inspirational verses during feasts and assemblies, and were commissioned to write praise poems and elegies for their noble patrons. They were also responsible for crafting scalding satires that served to hold the powerful accountable by threatening their reputations when they did not uphold the social contract.

We can identify several eras of Welsh Bardic Tradition, broken down into time periods and representing particular schools of thought, changing as Welsh culture changed:

- The Hengerdd Era (Old Songs) - 500s to the 1100s
- The Gogynfeirdd Era (Not-So-Early-Bards) - 1100s to the 1300s
- The Beirdd yr Uchelwyr Era (Bards of Nobility) - 1300s to the 1650s
- The Modern Era - 1650s to the present [8]

One of the earliest references to Ceridwen comes to us from the Black Book of Carmarthen, in verses attributed to Cuhelyn the Bard, circa 1100-1130:

> According to the sacred ode of Cyridwen, the Ogyrven of various seeds,—
> The various seeds of poetic harmony, the exalted speech of the graduated minstrel,
> Cuhelyn the wise, of elegant Cymraec,
> an exalted possession,
> Will skilfully sing [9]

In the earliest eras of Welsh Bardic Tradition, Ceridwen is characterized as *Mam yr Awen*, the Mother of Awen. She is appealed to as the origin of song and poetry, eloquence and excellence, and as the bestower of divine inspiration. Although we only have one full story that features Ceridwen, many references are made to her cauldron, her chair, and her role as the "*Ogyrven* of various seeds." Let's look at these attributes one by one to see what we they reveal to us about Ceridwen's nature.

---

[8] Hughes, *Cerridwen*, 42.

[9] Mary Jones (ed.), "The Ode of Cyridwen", *Black Book of Carmarthen IV*, in *The Celtic Literature Collective* https://www.maryjones.us/ctexts/bbc04.html [accessed 24 April 2025].

The Ogyrven

A word with many spellings in early bardic materials, *ogyrven* has proven to be an elusive word to understand. It is related to the modern Welsh word *gogyrfen* which has come to mean "letter; branch; symbol, element, spiritual form, personification." However, we must be careful as the *Geiriadur Prifysgol Cymru (Dictionary of the University of Wales,* hereafter abbreviated as GPC) notes that the word was a personal name taken from ancient poetry by the 18th century Welsh antiquarian Iolo Morgannwg and given new meanings by him. [10] In some works, Ogyrven as a personal name was used interchangeably with Ceridwen — while in others, it was used instead to describe her.

When we consult the GCP with a different spelling of the word, *ogrfen,* it is defined as "muse (Awen), inspiration; poetry." This aligns with the definition Marged Haycock gives for *gogyrwen* as "inspiration, a component of the Awen" in her seminal work *Legendary Poems from the Book of Taliesin.* [11] Yet, if this is truly the meaning of ogyrfen, it seems that its use in early Welsh poetry is often somewhat redundant at best, and inscrutable at worst, in as seen in the following verse from *Llyfr Taliesin*:

> Seith ugein ogyrfen, yssyd yn yr Awen.
> There are seven-score Ogyrfens in the Awen [12]

There are seven-score Awens in the Awen? Seven score components of inspiration in inspiration? What could this mean? There appears to be a mystery here.

---

[10] "gogyrfen." *Geiriadur Prifysgol Cymru Online*. Centre for Advanced Welsh and Celtic Studies, 2016. http://www.geiriadur.ac.uk [accessed: 15 April 2025].

[11] Haycock, *Legendary Poems from the Book of Taliesin,* 280.

[12] Mary Jones (ed.), *The Hostile Confederacy, Book of Taliesin VII*, in *The Celtic Literature Collective* https://www.maryjones.us/ctexts/t07.html [accessed 24 April 2025].

Recently, Welsh druid and author Kristoffer Hughes undertook his own translations of early Welsh poetry, particularly as concerns Ceridwen. Most of these works are written in Middle Welsh, and some of these pieces have never been translated into English before now. A native Welsh speaker, he addresses the enigma of the ogyrfen, writing:

> The prefix *ogr*, is a soft mutation of *gogr*, which is translated as 'sieve', or something that facilitates a sieving. Primarily in the Welsh language a *gogr* is a wooden framed tool with a fine mesh base used for winnowing and the separation of seeds from the seed body, or from smaller particles that are not required or considered as waste. The suffix '*fen*' can be taken to mean woman or womanly, whereas the suffix '*wen*' implies holy and blessed. There is little consistency of form in the old manuscripts, and the name has taken the same fate that is strikingly similar to the name of Cerridwen herself. The suffix fen is no longer seen in modern renditions, where the name has stabilized into the forms (G)Ogyrwen.
>
> The translation of Ogyrfen/Ogyrwen throughout all Bardic eras would appear thus: ***A woman who sieves, or the blessed and holy sieve.*** [13]

Hughes goes on to explore the idea of Ceridwen as, to use a title that reflects how I have come to understand her, She Who Winnows — the source of Awen who separates the worthy from the unworthy, the unprepared from the mysteries, and who serves as a filter to insure that the correct seeds will be incubated and empowered by the Awen. This is a revelatory hypothesis unlike those forwarded by previous scholars. It is grounded in etymology, and for which there are supportive reflections both in early Welsh poetry — such as the verses that link the Ogyrfen to various seeds — as well as in *Hanes Taliesin* (discussed in greater detail below) where Ceridwen, in the form of a black hen, devours the Awen-thief

---

[13] Hughes, *Cerridwen*, 56.

Gwion Bach who is hiding from her in the form of a seed on a threshing floor.

The Chair of Ceridwen

Another common attribute of Ceridwen, is her association with the *cadair* or "chair.' Like *ogyrven,* the word *cadair* also possesses many evocative meanings. In addition to meaning a seat, throne, and symbol of achievement or authority — to have a seat at a medieval court, as a bard would, was a reflection of one's importance — according to the GPC, *cadair* also means "a cluster, esp. of spreading branches or twigs", "a crib", the "udder of cow, mare, sheep", and a "principal or basic metre."[14] The use of words that are layered with multiple, interwoven meanings is emblematic of the art of the Welsh bards.

A primary source of early Welsh poetry is *Llyfr Taliesin* (*The Book of Taliesin*), the name given to a collection of poetic works dating to the 13th or 14th century, but which contains poems that scholars date back as far as the 9th century. One of those poems is called "Cadair Ceridwen", and in it the poet speaks as Ceridwen, describing how those who would seek to be honored for their poetic skill (to receive the bardic chair - *cadair*) must abide by her laws, ostensibly of meter (*cadair*) and rhyme:

> When are judged the chairs,
> Excelling them (will be) mine
> My chair, my cauldron and my laws,
> And my parading eloquence, meet for the chair.
> - "Cadair Ceridwen", *Llyfr Taliesin* [15]

---

[14] "cadair." *Geiriadur Prifysgol Cymru Online*. Centre for Advanced Welsh and Celtic Studies, 2016. http://www.geiriadur.ac.uk [accessed: 15 April 2025].

[15] Mary Jones (ed.), *The Chair of Cerridwen, Book of Taliesin XVI,* in *The Celtic Literature Collective.* https://www.maryjones.us/ctexts/t16.html [accessed 24 April 2025].

And so, we may read this as meaning when judged are the meters of poetry, those who are of Ceridwen — her bards, those who have come through her teachings, who have learned eloquence before her high seat and know the mysteries of her cauldron — will excel before all others who seek the honor of the bardic chair.

Whether in the past or the present, to win a bardic chair is a huge achievement in Welsh culture. In 1792, Iolo Morganwg rekindled the Gorsedd of the Bards on Primrose Hill in London. Emulating the bardic gatherings and competitions of medieval Wales, the Gorsedd became associated with the Welsh National Eisteddfod at the beginning of the 19th century, and their connection continues to this day. Even the words "Gorsedd" and "Eisteddfod" contain the Welsh root word for seat (*sedd*) in Welsh within them. [16]

The National Eisteddfod is a celebration of Welsh poetry, language, and culture. While it features many competitions across the arts, there are two poetry awards that make up the heart of the National Eisteddfod: the crowning of the bard (the winner of the free-verse competition) and the chairing of the bard (the winner of the metered verse completion). The opening of the event, and the granting of the poetry awards that close out the eight-day festival are carried out with great ritual pageantry that uplifts and centers Wales and the Welsh language. Hundreds of thousands of visitors attend the Welsh National Eisteddfod each year.

While this is a purely secular event, it is a testimony to the cultural significance of the Awen, that the Awenic symbol of the three rays /|\ called *Y Nod Cyfrin* ("The Mystic Mark") in Welsh, can be found emblazoned everywhere throughout the event. The presence of Ceridwen herself can still be felt in the judgment of those who compete annually for the top bardic prizes, especially as it concerns *Cadeirio'r Bardd,* the Chairing of the Bard. In addition to being hailed as *Y Prifardd* ("The Chief Bard"), the winner is given a literal,

---

[16] "eisteddfod." *Geiriadur Prifysgol Cymru Online*. Centre for Advanced Welsh and Celtic Studies, 2016. http://www.geiriadur.ac.uk [accessed: 15 April 2025].

locally-handcrafted wooden chair bearing the year and location of the Eisteddfod, and often featuring cultural symbols including Y Nod Cyfrin. Should the judges — themselves accomplished poets — find that none of the submission meet the standard of verse that they are looking for, they will decline to award the chair to anyone that year, rather than bestow it upon someone whose work was subpar — even if it was the best of the submissions.

Why? Perhaps this harkens back to the time when the bards knew to whom they had to answer for their art: She who sat in judgement of their rhymes and meter. It was no easy thing to become a bard. Not only did their education require them to memorize countless poems, songs, and lineages — a task of great importance for those entrusted with preserving and transmitting the whole of Welsh cultural wisdom through orality — but they were also required to learn a variety of poetic forms, and needed to be able to sing poetry in these forms *extempore*; that is to say, they had to improvise verses on the spot. All of this requires a high degree of mastery… and perhaps a little bit of magic.

The Cauldron of Inspiration

In addition to the powerful magical component inherent both in the rhyme and meter of verse and in the Welsh language itself, poetry was strongly entwined with prophecy in Welsh tradition. A bard needed to have access to the Awen — the creative, flowing breath of divine inspiration — so that they could tap into their mantic powers and speak things into being. In the early Welsh poem "Preiddeu Annwn" ("The Spoils of Annwn"), found in *Llyfr Taliesin*, we learn of a cauldron deep in the Welsh Otherworld (Annwn or Annwfn) from which poetry is uttered; it is in the keeping of nine maidens who kindle it with their breath. In this earliest extant Arthurian tale, potentially dating as far back as the 9th century in its written form, Arthur and three ships full of his men — including the famed bard Taliesin — launch a raid on the Otherworld in order to obtain this cauldron which belongs to the unnamed Chief of Annwn.

However, the modern scholar Sarah Higley posits that the poem isn't solely about Arthur's quest, but rather meant to be an allegory for the bardic process of attaining Awen. [17] This process required the bards to enter into the Welsh Otherworld, a place called *Annwn* or *Annwfn* — a name which translates either as "the not-world" or as "the very deep" — in order to retrieve a portion of Awen dispensed from this Otherworldly cauldron of poetry. It stands to reason that if the words used by bards in their poetry contained layered meanings, so too would their poetry as a whole... often referencing tales, figures, and —potentially — initiatory mysteries that only those of their order would understand. If that is the case here, meditating upon "The Spoils of Annwn" may reveal a mythic map that can guide an aspiring bardic seeker to connect with the Cauldron of Inspiration found in the very deepest part of themselves — a vessel very similar, if not the same, as the one possessed by Ceridwen.

We see Ceridwen's connection both with the Awen and with a cauldron of inspiration established very early on in Welsh literary tradition — a characteristic that persists for centuries, even as Ceridwen's reputation undergoes a bit of a revisioning, as we will see.

In his late 12th century book *The Description of Wales*, Giraldus Cambrensis or Gerald of Wales writes of those he called Awenyddion — the ones inspired — who would fall into deep trances and speak in strange streams of prophecy that they would not afterwards remember, although they afterwards said that their mouths became sweet with the taste of honey. Giraldus equates the gift of Awen inspiring these trance mediums with "the spirit of God."

---

[17] Sarah Higley, *"The Spoils of Annwn: Taliesin and Material Poetry"*, in *A Celtic Florilegium: Studies in Memory of Brendan O Hehir*, ed. by Kathryn A. Klar, Eve E. Sweetser, and Clair Thomas (Lawrence, MA: Celtic Studies Publications, 1966), pp. 43–53.

Similarly, the early 12th century Welsh court poet Llywarch ap Llywelyn, whose bardic name was Prydydd y Moch ("Poet of the Pigs"), wrote the following in one of his poems:

> Duw douyt dym ryt awen ber
> ual o beir kyrriduen
> The Lord God will give me the sweet Awen,
> as from the cauldron of Ceridwen[18]

That Ceridwen and her cauldron of poetic inspiration seemed to be able to exist side-by-side with the Christian God is worthy of note — as is the association of sweetness with the Awen, coming from two different sources, one prophetic and one poetic. This verse by Prydydd y Moch is also notable for being the first datable source directly linking Ceridwen with her cauldron.[19]

There are numerous references to experiences with Ceridwen that are suggestive of some sort of an initiatory encounter — of spending time in her court, of shapeshifting through a variety of forms, of experiencing life in a variety of time periods — in early Welsh poetry. This is most fully realized in the *Ystoria Taliesin* — a prose tale recounting the life of Taliesin — which also contains several, potentially older, poems including the following:

> I have obtained the muse from the cauldron of Caridwen;
> I have been bard of the harp to Lleon of Lochlin.
> I have been on the White Hill, in the court of Cynvelyn,
> For a day and a year in stocks and fetters,
> I have suffered hunger for the Son of the Virgin,
> I have been fostered in the land of the Deity,
> I have been teacher to all intelligences,
> I am able to instruct the whole universe.

---

[18] Bromwich, *Trioedd Ynys Prydein,* 313.
[19] Haycock, *Legendary Poems from the Book of Taliesin,* 312.

I shall be until the day of doom on the face of the earth;
And it is not known whether my body is flesh or fish.

Then I was for nine months
In the womb of the hag Caridwen;
I was originally little Gwion,
And at length I am Taliesin.[20]

And:

I have fled with vigour, I have fled as a frog,
I have fled in the semblance of a crow, scarcely finding rest;
I have fled vehemently, I have fled as a chain,
I have fled as a roe into an entangled thicket;
I have fled as a wolf cub, I have fled as a wolf in a wilderness,
I have fled as a thrush of portending language;
I have fled as a fox, used to concurrent bounds of quirks;
I have fled as a martin, which did not avail;
I have fled as a squirrel, that vainly hides,
I have fled as a stag's antler, of ruddy course,
I have fled as iron in a glowing fire,
I have fled as a spear-head,
of woe to such as has a wish for it;
I have fled as a fierce hull bitterly fighting,
I have fled as a bristly boar seen in a ravine,
I have fled as a white grain of pure wheat,
On the skirt of a hempen sheet entangled,
That seemed of the size of a mare's foal,
That is filling like a ship on the waters;
Into a dark leathern bag I was thrown,
And on a boundless sea I was sent adrift;

[20] Lady Charlotte Guest (trans.), "Taliesin", *The Mabinogion from the Welsh of the Llyfr Coch o Hergest (The Red Book of Hergest) in the Library of Jesus College, Oxford,* (London: Bernard Quaritch, 1877), pg. 483. https://sacred-texts.com/neu/celt/mab/mab32.htm [accessed: 15 April 2025].

Which was to me an omen of being tenderly nursed,
And the Lord God then set me at liberty.[21]

Perhaps these types of "I have been" verses are meant to establish bardic authority, allowing the poet to flaunt their knowledge and challenge the understanding of their peers and rivals. Alternatively, poetry of this kind may be intended to illustrate the need for the bard to be able to leave their form behind and become one with different aspects of nature — shifting as necessary in response to being challenged by Ceridwen.

Ceridwen the Witch

While Ceridwen the Muse lies at the heart of early to middle medieval Welsh bardic tradition, a cultural shift occurs during Y Beirdd yr Uchelwyr (The Bards of Nobility) Era. At this time, there was a deliberate movement away from Ceridwen and an attempt to disentangle bardism from her influence. In a passage from *Gwaith Iolo Goch* (*The Work of Iolo Goch*) recently translated into English by Kristoffer Hughes, the medieval bard Iolo Goch (1345-1397) writes of Ceridwen:

> "She is a ridiculous, stupid stock character, demonic and devilish, or so it would appear. And the image of her pulls on every familiar anti-feminine, anti-womanly motif; she is a loathsome, odious mock of a woman with her ugly, diseased and infectious, devouring and odious body, and her hideous consuming nature. No wonder that she should be mated with one who emulates so perfectly her demonic countenance. But let us now bury her and her ugly clubfoot and her magical strikes, this pointy wide-nostrilled hag, for we have lived long enough in the times of old Ceridfen."[22]

---

[21] Lady Charlotte Guest (trans.), "Taliesin", *The Mabinogion from the Welsh of the Llyfr Coch o Hergest (The Red Book of Hergest) in the Library of Jesus College, Oxford,* (London: Bernard Quaritch, 1877), pg. 475. https://sacred-texts.com/neu/celt/mab/mab32.htm [accessed: 15 April 2025].
[22] Hughes, Cerridwen, 49.

This movement to perpetuate a character assassination of Ceridwen, who was never depicted as a hag in previous accounts but rather as a mother in the prime of her fertility, is believed to be the origin of later perceptions and depictions of Ceridwen as an ugly hag and witch — a dabbler in sorcery and devourer of children, rather than the sacred source of the creative power of Awen. But even within the story of Taliesin, where she is at her witchiest and most terrifying, one need but scratch below the surface of the tale to find remnants of her former self and the role she played in bardic tradition. However, it is likely that the modern idea of Ceridwen as a Goddess of Witches and Witchcraft has its origins in this movement to discredit her and malign her femininity... for as far as the patriarchy is concerned, there is nothing worse than calling a woman an ugly hag , while accusing her of wielding demonic magic. After all, how could a *woman*, of all things, be the source of a force as powerful as the Awen?

The Story of Taliesin

For all of the allusions to Ceridwen found in early bardic poetry, she only appears in one extant tale which was collected relatively later than her first written reference from the early 12th century. *Ystoria Taliesin* (*The Story of Taliesin*) was recorded by Elis Gruffydd in his *Cronic o Wech Oesoedd* (*Chronicle of the Six Ages*) (NLW 5276D), written circa 1552. A variant version recorded by John Jones called *Hanes Taliesin (The History of Taliesin)*, appears in Peniarth Manuscript 111, dating to around 1607. As this tale (and its later variant) appear to have been collected from oral tradition, we do not know how long they may have existed in orality before being written down, although some scholars believe it can be traced back at least as far as the 9th century. [23]

In the story, Ceridwen is depicted as a witch or a sorceress, and Taliesin makes reference to having been nine months in the womb of Ceridwen the hag, making it clear that the The Beirdd yr

---

[23] Bromwich, *Trioedd Ynys Prydein*, 312.

Uchelwyr Era movement to discredit Ceridwen had taken root. Indeed, she almost completely disappears from bardic poetry after the publication of Iolo Goch's stinging rebuke of her. However, some of Ceridwen's older attributes — that of an initiatory muse — still remain embedded within the tale.

> First, I have been formed a comely person,
> In the court of Ceridwen I have done penance;
> Though little I was seen, placidly received,
> I was great on the floor of the place to where I was led;
> I have been a prized defence, the sweet muse the cause,
> And by law without speech, I have been liberated
> By a smiling black old hag, when irritated
> Dreadful her claim when pursued [24]

Hag or no, we learn that Ceridwen lives on the shores of Llyn Tegid with her husband, Tegid Foel, and two children — a beautiful daughter and a hideous son. Her actions to brew a draught of wisdom for her ill-aspected son sets into motion the transformation of Gwion Bach, her young assistant who — after stealing the three drops of wisdom for himself — was pursued by the enraged Ceridwen. The two engaged in a grand shapeshifting chase, with each taking on the form of different animals before Gwion was ultimately devoured by Ceridwen. Nine months later, the boy was reborn of Ceridwen, and grew up to become the great bard Taliesin — the paragon to whom all Welsh bards aspired.

Most scholars agree that this portion of the tale likely represents an encoded rite of initiation, detailing the process through which a student of bardcraft proved their worth through the trials and mysteries of Ceridwen. One might imagine that only those who were tested and found worthy became true bards able to access the Awen from Ceridwen's cauldron. Whether these trials were

---

[24] Lady Charlotte Guest (trans.), "Taliesin", *The Mabinogion from the Welsh of the Llyfr Coch o Hergest (The Red Book of Hergest) in the Library of Jesus College, Oxford,* (London: Bernard Quaritch, 1877), pg. 474. https://sacred-texts.com/neu/celt/mab/mab32.htm [accessed: 15 April 2025].

metaphorical or literally enacted ritual experiences is unknown, although some of the poems in *Llyfr Taliesin* hint at the kind of incubation rituals used by the poets of Ireland to obtain inspiration, supporting the idea that there may have been similar practices in Wales.[25] Whatever their nature, after passing through these experiences, the initiate would take on a bardic name — marking their transition into a new life, forever changed by having imbibed the elixir of wisdom. Through this rebirth, they become, like Taliesin, a child of Ceridwen.

Following the Mythic Map

I believe that the Story of Taliesin contains a mythic map that is a guide for undertaking a potent alchemical process of a spiritual nature. It lays out a pathway through a series of elemental and/or temporal transformations that culminates in a symbolic death and rebirth through the cauldron-alembic of Ceridwen's womb. It is through this process that the old self dies and a new self — blazing with the holy light of inspiration, and manifesting the Shining Brow of wisdom — is reborn, taking on a new life, a new form, and a new name.

The power of the story is the mythic map contained within it. It is a paradigm and process that lends itself to many different purposes, most especially the pursuit of Wisdom, the receipt of Awen, and as a means to enter into personal relationship with Ceridwen — the source of both. I have personally been in relationship with this tale from a psychospiritual perspective for decades, seeing it as a guide along the path to self-actualization, as well as a tool for self-evaluation. For me, using this mythic map as a guide to catalyze spiritual transformation is not in any way separate from the year and a day rarification process required to brew the elixir of wisdom by Ceridwen's cauldron. Indeed, the better we know ourselves — the more whole and healed we are — the more Awen our inner

[25] Patrick K. Ford, *Ystoria Taliesin* (Cardiff: University of Wales Press, 1992), 32.

vessels can hold, allowing us to direct that energy of creation in better service to the world.

What follows is a deconstruction of the main elements found in the only surviving tale we have of Ceridwen — a deconstruction that suggests one of many ways to be in relationship with the story of Taliesin... and with Ceridwen herself.

Child of Light, Child of Shadow

Let us begin by reflecting the story of Ceridwen and Taliesin within — seeing ourselves and the various components of our psyche represented in the characters that populate the tale. This does not mean that the story isn't sacred or that some of the personages within them are not divine, but it allows us to experience the events in the tale in a way that helps catalyze inner transformation. From a psychospiritual perspective then, we can see Ceridwen as representing our higher self — that whole, fully-integrated self that is in clear, unobstructed connection with the divine... which for me, is the Goddess Ceridwen herself. The two children of Ceridwen can be seen as representing the two parts of the Self — that which is revealed and conscious within us... and that which is buried in the Shadowed parts of the unconscious.

Her daughter, Creirwy, whose name may be derived from *crair* + *byw* "lively treasure, darling"[26], is named in the Welsh Triads as one of the Three Fair (Royal) Ladies of the Island of the Mighty (Triad 78) [27]. Within us, she represents all that is Sovereign, the parts of the self that dwell in beauty and bask, uninhibited, in the light of consciousness. Creirwy represents those parts of the Self which have been acknowledged and accepted; the potentials we have nurtured and actualized; and all of the parts of ourselves that know our love.

---

[26] Bromwich, *Trioedd Ynys Prydein,* 315.
[27] Ibid, 208.

In contrast, Ceridwen's son Morfran — meaning "cormorant", but which literally translates as "Sea Crow" in Welsh — is hideously ugly, such that he comes to be called Afagddu — "Utter Darkness." As Morfran, he can be seen as the messenger (raven) from the unconscious (the inner sea) that brings us hints of that which yet lies within us, unacknowledged and unseen — the role that the subconscious is meant to play. Within him, his deeper and most hidden self is Afagddu, who represents the Shadow Self. A vast hidden vessel that holds within it all that we have committed to the sea of forgetting — our trauma and shame and all of the things we have been taught to hide away lest we be cast out or punished, ridiculed or abandoned.

And yet, this Shadow is not our enemy. Indeed, its origins are often in our psyche's adaptations to external circumstances beyond our control; these ways of responding to the world around us have arisen within us to help us survive traumatic and painful circumstances. These adaptations manifest in in many ways: as heightened senses that have been sharpened on the whetstone of inconsistency and abuse that could turn violent at a moment's notice... as self-reliance woven from the threads of emotional and physical abandonment... as perfectionism wrought from the molten hot forge of constant criticism... as dissociation slicing through the veils of presence, cutting a gateway of escape from the horrors of the outside world.

In and of themselves, these are tools and weapons and structures of safety and resilience, crafted in the smithy of the unconscious. They were created to help us navigate painful situations and give us respite from a suffering we were often too young to understand — and which became internalized instead. We come to believe ourselves to be the cause of our suffering... believing ourselves unloved because we are unlovable, misunderstood because we are inscrutable, and broken because we are inherently flawed.

It is when the situations that catalyzed the creation of these adaptations have passed — either we have left them, or the perpetuators have moved on — and we wield these trauma-formed weapons against the world, that the ways we have been taught to look at the world and ourselves no longer reflect an accurate accounting of what is before us. Rather, we persist in seeing the world from the perspective of who we WERE rather than how it IS.... And, in doing so, our growth is curtailed by our Shadow, perpetuating patterns of perception and perspective that trigger these defense mechanisms that are not only no longer needed, but which hurt and limit us. We are still rooted in the abuse of the past.

The Shadow contains our outmoded psychological defense mechanisms: the things we were taught to hate about ourselves and our internalized shame. It holds the triggers for self-abuse through addictions, as well as self-deprivation. It sustains our belief in our unworthiness, our fear of loss and pain — and above all, our worry that others will see us as we see ourselves and will come to loathe and reject us as well.

Engaging Sacred Time

But Ceridwen loved both of her children — unconditionally. And the actions she takes to help her son can serve as guidance on our own paths into wholeness. She does not dwell upon that which is already beautiful, but fixes her eye instead on the suffering of Morfran. In the same way we cannot cut our Shadow off and throw it away, Ceridwen does not reject Afagddu or cast him out. Instead, she undertakes a complex, time and labor-consuming magical operation to create the Elixir of Wisdom for her son.

In many Celtic cultures, in order to rule as a chief or a king, one must be without blemish of body and mind. And so, in the tale, Ceridwen has reason to believe that the nobility and the rest of the world would be hard-pressed to accept her imperfectly-formed son who is described elsewhere in Welsh lore as having the visage of a demon, and being covered with coarse hair as thick as a stag. And so she aims to gift Afagddu with wisdom — a highly prized asset in

Welsh culture, and certainly one that will more than make up for her son's external appearance.

Similarly, we are called to bring the light of wisdom into the darkest regions of the Self; to seek knowledge of the truths within us — the pain, the wounding, the fear, the shame. Once obtained, this knowledge allows us to acknowledge the truth of the situations that created these within us. We can look at these parts of ourselves for what they truly are — for the wounds that are brought into the light can be healed, when possible, and can be accepted for what they are, if not. Light cleanses, sterilizes, and heals — and with that healing, comes empowerment and Sovereignty.

This process of inner illumination is not an easy one. It takes time, energy, and emotional resources — and often, requires assistance. Ceridwen undertook a period of study when she began the task of creating her brew. She researched tomes of natural science and alchemy, called the Books of Fferyllt in the tale, to craft her elixir. (*Fferyllt* is the Welsh name of the Roman poet Virgil, who came to be associated with magic and prophecy in the middle ages[28]. Based upon this name, *fferyllt* came to mean "chemist, druggist; alchemist; magician" in Welsh[29], suggesting that Ceridwen was consulting works of alchemy and magic, rather than any of the actual writings of the Roman writer.) Armed with this knowledge, she set her cauldron to boil "a brew of Inspiration and Science." [30]

Likewise, I believe that we are being called to observe the processes of nature around us, among them the ebb and flow of the tides, the increase and decrease of the moon's illumination, and the cyclic

---

[28] Juliette Wood, 'Virgil and Taliesin: The Concept of the Magician in Medieval Folklore', *Folklore*, 94.1 (1983), 91–104 (p. 97).

[29] "fferyllt". Geiriadur Prifysgol Cymru Online. Centre for Advanced Welsh and Celtic Studies, 2016. http://www.geiriadur.ac.uk [accessed: 15 April 2025].

[30] Lady Charlotte Guest (trans.), *The Mabinogion from the Welsh of the Llyfr Coch o Hergest (The Red Book of Hergest) in the Library of Jesus College, Oxford,* (London: Bernard Quaritch, 1877), pg. 471. https://sacred-texts.com/neu/celt/mab/mab32.htm [accessed: 15 April 2025].

round of the year. The story describes Ceridwen as having to add particular components to the brew at different times over the course of a year and a day before her labors were complete. Perhaps she gathered roots and bark and agents of decomposition in the winter, fragrant flowers and fresh mosses in the spring, hearty leaves and burgeoning fruits in the summer, ripened seeds and nuts and things undergoing the process of fermentation in the autumn — each ingredient having its own time and purpose, each phase of the process making way for those to follow.

This is an understanding that births true wisdom: that we are the sum of all that has come before — both personally and collectively — and who we are in the here and now is the starting point for the process of that the comes after. And just as she loves both Creirwy and Afagddu — both the light and the darkness — so Ceridwen teaches us to embrace both our ebb and our flow. To find as much value in times of dissolution as in times of creation To love all of the ages and phases of our life, for all are sacred, and even death gives way to renewal. But here, Ceridwen applies her knowledge of these patterns and harnesses them to create a brew that will bestow all wisdom upon the person who drinks of it.

The Great Good and the Little Innocent

However, there was much work to be done, while she worked to gather and add ingredients at the proper times and continuously renewed the water for her brew, even Ceridwen needed help with this process. She enlisted the aid of an old blind man named Morda ("Great Good") and a young servant boy by the name of Gwion Bach ("Little Innocent"). The blind man was tasked with feeding the fire that kept her cauldron boiling, while the child was charged with stirring the constantly bubbling brew.

Think what we can learn from this. That part of ourselves that seeks the wisdom of transformation must acknowledge that this process is an ongoing one, requiring us to bring forth different parts of ourselves in their own time because different facets of ourselves become accessible in different measures. Further, the consistent addition of water — the medium in which the brew is being crafted — is related to the unconscious, memory, and emotion... those glassy inner surfaces that facilitate this ongoing process of inner reflection and self-revelation.

It seems strange that a blind man would be the one to feed the fire, but as he represents the Great Good, perhaps he is the conscious trust we must have in ourselves to undertake this process at all. An elderly man, he represents the Jungian notion of the Senax, or sage — one whose wisdom derives from their experience of life. Perhaps we are being called to look to the past and to remember all that we have been through and survived, and draw upon these experiences to support our Will — to keep the fire within us directed towards catalyzing change.

And the young boy Gwion Bach? He is innocent and untested, true — but he has the strength and resilience to stir the cauldron — to allow the components of the brew to rise up to the surface and break down to become part of the broth. Perhaps he is the unspoiled part of ourselves — the *puer eternus* or perpetual youth — untouched by the ravages of time and the cruelty of circumstance. His name is cognate with the Welsh word "gwyn" meaning "white, shining, holy" — a word often associated with or embedded in the names of divinities in Welsh tradition, like the -*wen* in Ceridwen. Perhaps he is the sacred part of ourselves that is agitating for wholeness, bringing things up from the depths of the self to the surface of our consciousness, working towards transformation and actualization.

This is hard work, needing consistency, dedication, and time. The brewing process itself takes a year and a day — a sacred time outside of time, where the extra day represents a liminality, forming a threshold between the worlds through which the essence of the Otherworld enters this world. In this case it takes the form of the three shining drops of wisdom that emerge from the cauldron, freed from the poison of all that is left behind.

Likewise, we are called to undertake a process of inner distillation, so that we may bring the light of consciousness into the depths of the Shadow, thus permitting us reclaim the illumination of sovereignty from the limitations that poison us and prevent us from being whole.

And when the lightning flash of understanding comes, we are forever changed. Like the cauldron when the brewing process is complete, our old form cracks and breaks; we have outgrown its outmoded limitations, and the toxicity within us is released. The self-knowledge that comes through the revelation of our truth is reclaimed.

The Great Chase

The story tells us that on the final day of the brewing of her elixir, Ceridwen grew weary. Before going to her rest, she placed her son before the cauldron so that he would be able to receive the three drops of wisdom should they emerge before she returned. It is at this point that the two versions of the tale diverge. In the older version recorded by Ellis, when the brew is finished, Gwion pushes Morfran aside to receive the three drops of wisdom for himself. In the later version, the drops accidentally splash on Gwion's finger, burning him. He instinctively places his burnt finger in his mouth and thus receives the wisdom meant for Morfran.

I personally prefer the agency Gwion shows in the first version, while the second version appears to have been influenced by a similar tale from Irish tradition. In that story, after waiting seven years to catch a salmon which had been feeding on the nuts from nine hazel trees surrounding the Well of Segais, a druid sets his young apprentice named Demne to oversee the cooking of the fish. When the skin of the salmon of wisdom begins to bubble, the boy presses it in with his thumb and burns himself. As with Gwion, Demne pops his burnt thumb in his mouth to soothe the pain and receives the wisdom the druid had been seeking. Demne grows to become the poet-warrior Fionn mac Cumhaill, who was able to receive Imbas — the Irish analog of Awen — by putting his thumb in his mouth. There are many connections between these two stories; not only did both boys receive the inspiration intended for another, and change their names as a result of this shift, but the name Fionn is cognate to that of Gwion, in that they both have at their root the words for "white, shining, and holy."

However he received them, upon taking in the three drops of wisdom, Gwion was immediately filled with the knowledge that Ceridwen was going to be furious with him when she learned what happened, and so he runs from her home. As he does so the cauldron splits in two — spilling the poisonous remains of the brew everywhere; it befouls the water of a nearby stream, killing the horses that drank from it. The sound of the breaking cauldron startles Ceridwen awake, and she soon discovers what has happened. Gwion uses his newfound wisdom to change his shape into that of a swift hare. However, Ceridwen also has the ability to shape-shift and, turning herself into a greyhound, she begins an enraged pursuit of the boy who took the elixir of wisdom that was meant for her son.

What follows is a series of animal transformations that are believed to represent the initiatory process of a Welsh bard. We do not know if these are meant to represent a metaphorical pathway of training and evolution in the bardic arts, or if there was a literal ritual testing that a postulant would have to undertake in order to prove their ability and worth — or both. However, the power of the story is that its symbolism remains potent even from the perspective of a modern-day spiritual seeker.

While Gwion has taken something that was not meant for him, he is forced to embark upon a journey that tests his skill — forcing him to not only test his limitations and adapt to the challenges resulting from Ceridwen's pursuit of him, but to prove his worthiness of the elixir — to earn what he had received. For knowledge alone is not enough; it becomes wisdom only when it is actively applied and mastery obtained. It must be integrated, catalyzing change in every aspect of the self; only then is it truly won.

The pursuit of Gwion by Ceridwen can be interpreted in many ways. From a psychospiritual perspective, this entire process began because Ceridwen wished to bring the light of wisdom to Utter Darkness. To obtain this wisdom, a process of inner distillation spanning a year and a day was necessary to separate three shining drops of inspiration from the limitations of the Shadow. This alchemical process resulted in the breaking of the old form, and the release of the toxic dregs remaining behind. If we see ourselves now as Gwion, the innocent who is forever changed by the wisdom received, it is now time for us to integrate this change in all aspects of our being — helped by the Mother of Awen who challenges us at every step. It is through this journey of transformation through the elements — and the associated aspects of the self — that the process of integration is revealed.

Hare and Greyhound

Gwion runs from Ceridwen's home in the form of a hare, but she pursues him in the form of a swift greyhound and is soon nipping at his heels. Representing the element of Earth, this portion of the Great Chase addresses the way we are in relationship with our physical world. In what ways have the illusions of our Shadow taken root in the physical plane — how has it manifested in the situations of our lives, in the limitations we have accepted about ourselves, and the way we move through the world? The challenge of Ceridwen is to bring illumination to these things and, once revealed, to use the creative energies of her Awen to affect change.

Salmon and Otter

Although Ceridwen almost takes Gwion into her jaws, he casts himself into the lake and transforms into a swift, silver salmon. Undaunted by his efforts to escape her, Ceridwen follows closely behind him, continuing her pursuit of him as an otter. Representing the element of Water, this portion of the Great Chase addresses the way we are in relationship with our emotional world. In what ways have the illusions of our Shadow seeped into the emotional plane — how does it affect our feelings and relationships with others, the people and projects and outcomes to which we are attached, and to what we pour out the resources of our inner vessel? If these things are not in alignment with our Sovereign self, Ceridwen calls for us to change.

Wren and Hawk

Narrowly avoiding her insistent grasp, Gwion flings himself into the air — taking on the form of a wren. But Ceridwen will not be denied her vengeance, and it is not long before she resumes the chase, slicing through the sky as a sharp-taloned hawk. Representing the element of Air, this portion of the Great Chase addresses the way we are in relationship with our mental world. In what ways have the illusions of our Shadow billowed into the mental plane — how has it affected our thought processes, perspectives and beliefs; how has it clouded the lenses through which we see and understand the world; and how does it prevent us from communicating with clarity? Lady of eloquence, wisdom, and foresight... Ceridwen challenges us to change.

Seed and Hen

Increasingly panicked and growing weary, Gwion struggles to evade Ceridwen's grasp while searching for someplace to hide as the pair fly over the countryside. At last spying the open door of a barn, Gwion flies down and changes himself into a grain of wheat, hiding among the seeds and the chaff on the threshing floor. He is closely followed by Ceridwen, who transforms herself into a black-feathered hen. Patiently and methodically, she scratches and pecks at the winnowed wheat until she finds him at last — and swallows him whole. Representing the element of Fire, this portion of the Great Chase addresses the way we are in relationship with our energetic world. In what ways have the illusions of our Shadow impacted our ability to express our will, affected what impels us to action or prevents us from acting, and determined how and where we expend our energy? When we are not acting in right relationship with ourselves and others, Ceridwen challenges us to change.

Gwion and Taliesin

The seed that is Gwion takes root in Ceridwen's womb, and she gives birth to a son nine months later. Gwion's last and greatest transformation is to leave his old self behind and be reborn of the Goddess of Inspiration herself. Representing the element of Spirit, this final portion of the Great Chase addresses the way in which we are in relationship with the Divine — and with our actualized Self. In what ways have the illusions of our Shadow created disconnection with the spiritual plane — how has it prevented us from accepting the whole of who we are, colored the truth of our connection with Source, and allowed us to believe that we are not worthy of being in divine relationship? Unconditionally loving every part of us, Ceridwen challenges us to change.

It is this last portion of this cycle of transformation that is defined by its ability to help the whole become integrated — and which calls for us to surrender to the will of the divine. For when Ceridwen the Hen eats Gwion the Seed, she reveals an important aspect of her nature. She is the Devouring Mother, the Holy Sow that eats what is rotten and corrupted so that healing can occur and we can be reborn — renewed, experienced, and bringing the wisdom we've now earned with us into the next phase of our lives.

Thrice Born

When Ceridwen gives birth to the transformed Gwion, there is a terrible moment where her anger is renewed. She considers destroying the infant, but softens in the face of his beauty as well as the realization that he represents what this process set out to do — to give her a son who has been infused with all wisdom. But the reborn Gwion's work is not yet done, and on the 29th of April

Ceridwen releases him out into the world once more; she places him in a leather bag and sets him afloat on the sea in a coracle.

After 40 years of being carried along by the waves, the infant's coracle is found in a salmon weir on May Eve by the Welsh prince Elfin. Frustrated after a day of empty nets, Elfin pulls the coracle from the waters and slices open the squirming leather bag he finds within the craft. Upon seeing the baby within, the prince exclaims, "Behold, the radiant brow!" And this is how the infant received the name Taliesin — Radiant Brow, glowing with the mark of his great wisdom. This paragon to which all other bards aspired was this thrice born child of Ceridwen — born once as Gwion Bach, born again from the womb of Ceridwen, and then birthed a third time into the hands of Elfin who freed him from the womb-like leather bag, bringing the great bard into this world once more after a long journey from the Otherworld.

His bright brow can be seen to represent the illumination of his integrated wisdom, which accompanies him into his new life. Likewise, when we unearth those precious morsels of truth within us ... when we are blessed with the transformational energies of the Awen through our inner strivings and outer dedication to the Divine Muse, Ceridwen... our work is not complete. Instead, the cyclic pathway revealed by the mythic map embedded in the narrative of *Ystoria Taliesin* demonstrates that we too must go back out into the world — and back down into ourselves — so that we may engage with this alchemical process anew. However, as we do so, we are able to bring our newly-liberated wisdom with us, which will serve to inform and guide us through the work of this inner distillation and integration with ever-increasing clarity and trust in our process.

On What Is Carried

From the moment Gwion Bach takes possession of the drops of inspiration, and heads on out the door, the elixir's intended recipient disappears from the narrative of the story. So what becomes of Morfran/Afagddu? Does Ceridwen begin another round of brewing to ensure that her first son receives the wisdom she desired for him?

It appears not.

Instead, he seems to have found his place in the world even without his mother's assistance. Morfran grows up to be one of King Arthur's knights, becoming a fierce and loyal warrior. He is counted among the three survivors of Arthur's final battle at Camlan; it is said that due to his ugliness, no-one attacked him on the battlefield, believing him to be a demon. Like his sister Creirwy, Morfran is mentioned in *Trioedd Ynys Prydein* (*The Triads of the Island of Britain*), but where she was lauded for her beauty, it is his ugliness that causes him to be remembered as one of the Three Slaughter-Blocks of the Island of Britain, as well as One of the Three Irresistible Knights of Arthur's Court. His appearance was so disarming on the battlefield, his opponents could not bring themselves to fight him and he used their hesitation against them. Perhaps Morfran possessed some degree of wisdom after all. He was able to take that part of him that his divine mother deemed to be his greatest flaw and turn it into his greatest strength.

Likewise, when we are engaging with the work of spiritual alchemy that helps us transform aspects of our personal Shadow into the wisdom drops of Sovereignty, we may find that there are parts of ourselves that may never be healed — but it does not mean that they cannot be mastered or overcome in a different way. The things that cannot be changed in our lives are often things that we can learn to carry with grace and self-acceptance. When we walk a spiritual path, the wise person learns to seek wholeness rather than perfection. And what a beautiful lesson it is to know that our self-actualization is not reliant on our purity, but rather on our ability to see ourselves as we truly are — both the sovereignty and the shadow — and love ourselves just the same.

To Sing the Awen

Whether aspiring bard or spiritual seeker, creator of poetry or paintings or children or communities — there are many reasons for us to seek the Awen... many ways that we can become catalysts for change. Ceridwen calls us to become our best selves — to become a whole and holy vessel able to be filled with the creative force of her divine inspiration, and able to pour it out in service to the world and inspire others in return. May her prophetic poetry ever pass through our lips, her masterful meters guide the rhythms of our lives, and her sacred sieve help us to separate the seeds of our sovereignty from the chaff of what no longer serves us.

And so, to Holy Ceridwen, let us sing:

> Lady of the Cauldron, fill us with your Streams of Illumination so that we may find the depth of our vessels and test the true nature of our mettle — so that, in your service, we may be active co-creators of this world.
>
> Holy Woman of Song, teach us the art of transformation so that we may become all that we are meant to be, harnessing the cycles of change as our old form breaks and we surrender to your will — in pursuit of your wisdom, in pursuit of our wholeness.
>
> Sacred Muse, inspire us to peer into the Utter Darkness of our limitations so that we may reveal the Fairest Treasure within us – the divine potential of our souls.
>
> Mother of Awen, warm us with the flame of your unconditional love, as we strive towards excellence and seek to reborn of you — our brows ablaze with your holy light.

Bibliography

Bromwich, Rachel, *Trioedd Ynys Prydein: The Welsh Triads* (Cardiff: University of Wales Press, 2006).

Ford, Patrick K. (ed.), *Ystoria Taliesin* (Cardiff: University of Wales Press, 1992).

Guest, Lady Charlotte, *The Mabinogion from the Welsh of the Llyfr Coch o Hergest (The Red Book of Hergest) in the Library of Jesus College, Oxford* (London: Bernard Quaritch, 1877).
https://sacred-texts.com/neu/celt/mab/mab00.htm.

Haycock, Marged, *Legendary Poems from the Book of Taliesin*, 2nd ed. (Aberystwyth: Centre for Medieval Studies, 2015).

Higley, Sarah, "The Spoils of Annwn: Taliesin and Material Poetry", in *A Celtic Florilegium: Studies in Memory of Brendan O Hehir*, ed. by Kathryn A. Klar, Eve E. Sweetser, and Clair Thomas (Lawrence, MA: Celtic Studies Publications, 1966), pp. 43–53.

Hughes, Kristoffer, *Cerridwen: Celtic Goddess of Inspiration* (Woodbury, MN: Llewellyn Worldwide, 2019).

Jones, Mary, 'Cerridwen', in *Celtic Encyclopedia*,
https://www.maryjones.us/jce/cerridwen.html [accessed 16 April 2025].

Jones, Mary (ed.), *The Ode of Cyridwen, Black Book of Carmarthen IV*, in *The Celtic Literature Collective.*
https://www.maryjones.us/ctexts/bbc04.html [accessed 24 April 2025].

Jones, Mary (ed.), *The Hostile Confederacy, Book of Taliesin VII*, in *The Celtic Literature Collective.*
https://www.maryjones.us/ctexts/t07.html [accessed 24 April 2025].

Jones, Mary (ed.), *The Chair of Cerridwen, Book of Taliesin XVI*, in *The Celtic Literature Collective.*
https://www.maryjones.us/ctexts/t16.html [accessed 24 April 2025].

Wood, Juliette, 'Virgil and Taliesin: The Concept of the Magician in Medieval Folklore', *Folklore*, 94.1 (1983), 91–104.

Cerridwen

Elizabeth SolArt

What Foolishness is This? Cerridwen's Cauldron is for All of Us

Carolyn Lee Boyd

"What foolishness is this?" Cerridwen's voice railed in exasperation and anger over the drone of my inner voice as I reread Her myth. Not waiting for my reaction, She continued:

"I look out over your world and see how my gift of inspiration has been misused, the opportunity for divine creation taken away from most people in your age of celebrity and the idolatry of fame and fortune, leading to a dulling of your world and imaginative catastrophe. My story as you have heard it has beauty and meaning but perhaps it is now time to change perspectives and see it also from another point of view. Let me tell you a second version of the story.

"When my son was born, he was called Afagdu, 'Utter Darkness.' Because he did not look like other children, it was feared he would never be accepted by society. What child is ugly to a mother? If no one else would love him, I would make up for it by loving him a thousand times more, not by having him drink some overboiled elixir.

"Brew up a potion from herbs to give him brilliance and wisdom, they said. Do they think that I do not have the power to see into the future, that I do not know what would happen? That evil servant Gwion stole the concoction. And the cauldron burst open and poisoned the world. Or so they thought. I did indeed make a mixture of herbs, but not the one they believed.

"They said I chased Gwion aided by my friends who let me borrow their bodies, the greyhound, an otter, a hawk, and a hen. Knaves. Why would I chase someone who stole something that can never be stolen, if indeed it had been genius? Or that, in reality, was worthless to him? Did they think I couldn't make more potion if I had wanted to, if the potion had been what gave the gift of the muses?

"They say I ate the traitor Gwion as a grain of wheat and gave birth to him as the great bard Taliesin. Who thinks I could be forced to unwillingly give birth to such a one? Gwion escaped our household and made up a tale to explain his odd origin when he wished to be perceived as a great bard of mythical origins.

"I did give birth when I heard the story he had conjured, but not to a being, but rather to a revelation that inspiration belongs not to the gods and their chosen elite, but rather to all. Brilliance comes not from memorizing hundreds of stories, poems, and genealogies like the bards, but from hard-won life experience and the knowledge it brings that love is our only true muse.

"But I let the story continue to be told far and wide. I did not speak against it because it uttered helpful truths, but here is another beneficial true story. How much love must a mother have for her child to carefully forage and prepare the herbs, then place them in a gigantic pot, and ensure they are carefully tended for a year and a day? Would not Afagdu have received from this not false genius, but the knowledge that, though he was reviled by everyone else, his mother deeply loved him? Might this have not given him the confidence he needed to find the virtuosity within himself to write dazzling poetry and be the most celebrated bard in history had not Gwion intervened? Might his name Utter Darkness instead have meant the womb inside the Earth and within each of us where we take the manifestations of love and make them into artistic jewels that shine, sometimes in their terribleness, sometimes in their joy of being? Might not the works of Gwion, later known as Taliesin, actually have been those of Afagdu, the credit stolen by history once both were long gone from the human realm?

"When the cauldron broke, it was not poison that spilled across the world, it was imagination and artistry. The gods had wanted the genius of creation to be under their control, to be only for those they chose, with no love, grace, or passion for life's everyday beauty. They thought that since I was immortal, too, I would be their servant and let Gwion steal the potion. But I did not, nor did they know that the potion was nothing more than random herbs and that the love of its making was the magic.

"Instead, once Afagdu had been made luminous by the mixture made possible by my motherly love, I spread the potion over the whole world, into those places that ordinary humans, as the gods call them, (Are there ordinary humans? No, anyone who survives life as a mortal is extraordinary) venture but never the gods. I infused inspiration into the daily and seemingly mundane acts of romance, into human cries of grief heard only by themselves and those close to them, into the warmth of small acts of friendship, into the billion exchanges between parents and children that happen every day, into the often silent human yearning for the sea and forest. It is now inextricably part of everything on Earth that bridges humans to other elements of their cosmos, all that helps them find and fulfill their place in the realm of mortality. The bounty of the cauldron was not a potion, but love and the knowledge of how to use it to create works of beauty, wisdom, and truth out of the struggles and delights of daily human life.

"Taking inspiration from the tyranny of the gods and giving it to humanity is how I now choose to use my own enlightenment." And then Her voice was silent.

In the 21st century's world it can seem as if Cerridwen's cauldron is soon to run dry. We look into it hoping a drop has remained, weary and exhausted by the apathy, fear, hate, misery, and despair all around us. What can we possibly create to remake such a planet? But look, Cerridwen is now brewing a special potion just for us, made from our passionate desire to make a better world, from our looking at our sisters and seeing in their eyes just enough fortitude to put together three drops of hope, from our own love of self that has survived all the traumas as well that which has been nourished by all the love we have received in our lives. It is fragrant with roses and lilies for beauty, basil to banish negativity, bee balm for the blessing of the fairies, daisies for luck, lavender for healing body and soul, marjoram to offer solace for grief, spearmint for courage, and so many more. What else could we need?

Look into it and see what is missing from your life and your work. Put in your thumb and taste three drops. It is not only allowed but encouraged. You might be surprised at what comes out – perhaps not what you wanted but for sure just what you need. Our world may seem short on love at this moment. When we draw on our loving relationships to be inspired, we not only bring into being artistry of genius, but we make more love when it spreads to everyone who experiences what we have conjured and constructed in an ever-growing web of love and life.

Now it is your choice how you use Cerridwen's gift to you. When you seek inspiration, will you look to the outside world to see what others desire you to make or will you seek inside yourself for what you love most? Will you use it to strengthen and make radiant the affiliations between yourself and those beings and places you cherish based on what you have learned during your days here on Earth, making all of Creation shine? Cerridwen is here to give you all you need to do the work you were born on this Earth to do.

She made Her choice and now it is our turn to make ours.

Sources:

Original story of Cerridwen's cauldron from Monaghan, Patricia, *The New Book of Goddesses and Heroines*, St. Paul, MN: Llewellyn Publications, 2000, pp. 82-83.

Herb correspondences from the *Herb Chart* of the Salem Witch Museum, Salem, MA.

Eternal Alchemy

Maria Kefalogianni

The porosity of this being
in the heat of this cauldron
invites me willingly
to let my body become ashes
in the thick smoke of ancestral fire—
eternal dust in the swell of blazing flames.

I invite the world's pouring pain
to alchemize in my cosmic womb,
transforming into potent medicine;
liquified magic once destroyed
and forgotten by humanity.

But, my dear one,
this potion I am drunk in
is carved within my veins,
fleshed upon my skin—
Inscribed in the unturned pages
of my pre-written books,
poetry and prose.

When the weather changes
and pours down rain,
I let the coolness of my tears
wet my inner longing.
Kneeling on the Earth,
I become a sculpture from my own ashes.

At will, I let myself become
malleable clay.

This melting
is my deliverance.

Cerridwen's Cauldron

Andrea Redmond

Stirring the Cauldron: How a Visit to Lake Bala Changed My Life

Lyn Thurman

In September 2019, I found myself in a life that felt as though it was on autopilot. My days were predictable, and although I wasn't unhappy, I felt a stirring inside me that I couldn't quite place. It was then that Cerridwen entered my life.

I took a spur-of-the-moment trip to North Wales with my husband and daughter. I wanted to go to Norfolk in England but he, having birthday decision privileges, chose a small, Welsh seaside village to spend a couple of days. Whenever we have the opportunity to stay away, I like to pack every moment full. This mini-break was no different and, as I didn't think we'd be back any time soon, I wanted to make sure we could say we had experienced as much as we could in the time we had.

There were beaches to walk, ancient copper mines to explore and waterfalls to admire. There was one place though that called me more than any – Llyn Tegid or Lake Bala, nestled in beautiful Eryri (Snowdonia). It is here that the tale of Cerridwen and Taliesin takes place. It's said that her cauldron bubbled with the brew of inspiration on a small island in the middle of the lake. The potion was meant for her son but Gwion Bach, a boy who had been stirring the pot for a year, accidentally took three drops of the potion and thus began a shapeshifting, rebirth journey into Taliesin, the most famous bard of Wales.

Lake Bala is stunningly beautiful. When we arrived at the shores, on our whistle-stop tour of North Wales, it took my breath away. There is no little island in the lake, but you can feel the magic. It seeps into the pores of your skin. It whispers in your ear. It takes hold of your heart and won't let go.

On this sunny, early autumn afternoon, I sat by the lake and stared out over the still waters. My husband and daughter were off exploring, and I was savouring the quietness. It had been a very difficult few years with challenging family dynamics and financial strain. I was exhausted, often anxious, and I needed this small respite. I kept my gaze on the lake and let my mind wander to Cerridwen. She is a goddess of transformation and rebirth, and the keeper of the cauldron of Awen, the potion of divine inspiration. A deep sense of peace washed over me, as if the Goddess was comforting me, enveloping me in Her energy.

I wanted to feel peace. I wanted to be able to breathe deeply and have space in my life for magic to unfold. I wanted to be inspired by life, not dully getting through the days. I wanted what Cerridwen offered. Like Gwion Bach, I too was being called to transform, to stir the cauldron of my own life.

A while later, my husband joined me on the shore. He sat next to me and I blurted out: "I want more of this. Let's move here."

To my surprise, he agreed.

As long as our daughter would be in agreement, we gave ourselves a six-month deadline to sell our house on the south coast of England and find somewhere to live in North Wales. Before I left Lake Bala, I picked up several white pebbles from the shore to keep as a reminder of Cerridwen and the goal to move 275 miles away in search of magic.

The spell had been cast but would it manifest?

I haven't moved house where the process was easy and without any challenges. Whenever we hit a roadblock, and there were several big ones, I would make a point of doing whatever I could to get back on track and then I would walk it off. My husband and I walked miles during this time, becoming aware that our movement was linked to the movement of our goal. Each step was a manifestation of my intention to keep moving, both literally and spiritually. And almost without fail, during or after our walks, something had shifted. I'd receive an email or phone call that put us back in alignment with our intention.

As 2020 came into focus, it was beginning to look as if our move might be possible. We had a buyer for our house and all we needed to find somewhere to move to. We found a house, they accepted our offer but then pulled out once we were heading back home to England. A backup house, the very first one I'd seen online, was a possibility and our offer was accepted. It was an Edwardian, terraced cottage, full of character with fireplaces and high ceilings.

By the middle of March 2020, society's landscape had changed, and it was becoming increasingly apparent that a pandemic would delay, if not halt, our moving plans. There was nothing we could do so we let the dream go, leaving it in the hands of the Goddess.

Exactly six months to the day of my visit to Cerridwen at Lake Bala, I received a phone call from my solicitor. We're going to exchange contracts. It's all a go. You'll be moving on Monday.

That call came on a Friday afternoon. We weren't packed up. We didn't have transportation to take our belongings to Wales.

To say it was probably the most exhausting weekend of my life is an understatement. We hired a van; we filled it with boxes and plants and personal possessions. We were ready to begin our new adventure in the dark hours of that Monday.

Truly in limbo, straddling the liminal space of having officially sold our house but not yet purchased our new one (the UK house buying system is full of strange quirks like this) and hurtling up the motorway, our mobile phones all sounded with an alert.

In ten hours, the UK would be in a national lockdown.

We had all our possessions in the back of a rental truck that had to be returned the next day. We didn't know if we had a house to move into. And, like the rest of the world, we didn't have a clue what a lockdown would truly mean.

But what to do? Take a deep breath and keep moving forward. Moving, always moving. A lesson I had learnt well from Cerridwen. It was as if movement was the stick that stirred the magic cauldron, and if you wanted to receive Her blessings then you'd better keep in motion.

We made it. We picked up the keys, unpacked and eventually allowed a sigh of relief to leave our lips. And with that sigh was a whisper of gratitude to Cerridwen for the inspiration and assistance in bringing me to this new country full of wonder, beauty and tales of magic.

The white pebbles I picked up on my first visit to Lake Bala sit on my bedside table. I returned to Bala, after lockdown restrictions were lifted, and bought a print of Cerridwen by a local artist at the Goddess Temple that sits in my dining room on a mantlepiece above the fireplace.

I have found the peace and space I craved. And through that, I never feel far away from Cerridwen or her cauldron. Her lessons have become a quiet guide in my moments of doubt, reminding me that life's magic is always within reach—if I keep moving. Now, as I look out over the Welsh hills from my home, I still feel her presence, urging me to stay inspired and embrace life's unfolding journey. My life, although still a work in progress, is now fuelled by creativity and transformation, and I am beyond grateful for that seemingly ordinary day in Wales when the Goddess filled my heart and spoke to my spirit. Life hasn't been the same since—and I wouldn't want it any other way.

The Cauldron

Sharon Smith

While walking in the forest deep
I came upon a Cauldron Black
As Black as Night
As Black as Death
As perfect as
A Baby's Breath.

And there was SHE a-stirring fast
The Brew within Her Cauldron Pot,
First Deosil
Then Widdershins
The Brew within
The Cauldron spins.

I did not know who stirred the Pot,
I'd never seen the likes of Her:
A Wizened Crone?
A Maiden fair?
A Mom with milk
Spewed in Her hair?

She seemed somehow to be the Three
I called to Her and asked Her Name
She stirred and stirred
And stirred, and then
She said, "My name
is Cerridwen."

I caught my breath and held it still,
She looked at me with eyes as deep
As Time itself
And once again
She softly spoke
A word: "Awen."

And then Her breath enveloped me,
Her voice a cantillation raised;
"Awen, Awen,"
Thus chanted She,
And "Awen" came
alive in me.

Then She and I, and I and She
became as One at Cauldron Black;
I helped Her stir,
She helped me see
That Magick is
Alive in me.

Life and Breath and Spirit call
From deep within Her Sacred Brew;
She held a bit
For me to taste,
And cautioned not
A drop to waste.

I gladly sipped it from Her spoon,
Like honeyed wine, it warmed my soul;
She opened my eyes
And helped me see
Cerridwen's
Sacred Mystery.

Transformation is Her fire;
Initiation is Her fuel;
She gave me Life;
She taught me Death;
She birthed in me
The Awen Breath.

She taught me how to change my skin,
And walk through Darkness without fear;
The challenges
That I must face,
I do so with
Cerridwen's grace.

O Goddess of the Cauldron Black;
O Mother of the Broken Child;
You know deep pain
and anguish too;
Your tears are part
Of your own Brew.

Awen, Awen, Awen, Awen —
I sing it oft' when morning breaks;
Your Pain and Tears,
Transmuted then,
Bring healing grace,
O, Cerridwen!

Awen

Betsy Long

Cerridwen's Cauldron

Esther Marcella Hoffmann

I sleep in the lap of Her lake,
and wake with night's ivory light
on the nape of my neck.

There is a path back into the forest.
Moon and sun stones alternate on the way
to Her cottage.

Rounding the garden, whiffs of
rosemary, lavender, lemon-thyme,
I follow the glowing of a fire.
I halt when I see Her.

Gentle potential, a nudge
from the head of the Great White Sow,
I step forward toward Awen.

She swirls a twilight-colored liquid,
adds unearthed bundles of herbs,
and jars of esoteric flowing.

Three drops are transformation; one more is poison.
I must die for the woman I am becoming.
She offers me the potion.

So, I may speak the languages of flames,
teach the speeches of breezes.
So, I listen to green singing on leaves,
take dictate of the dreams of streams.

The three, salt-clarity, sweet-courtesy, grit-honesty,
drip under my tongue, as She hands
me a blank scroll.

My temples hollow into the hallowed hall,
where She whispers the ancestral secrets of Earth,
entrusts me with the verses of the Universe.
I, trembling, dedicate these pages,
and my being, to Her musings.

Creatrix: Goddess of Creation

Reti Toriella

The Love of a Mother

Susan Morgaine

Like Ceridwen, I am the mother of a daughter and a son.

What would you do for your challenged son.
What could you do that has not been done.
What have you done to bring him clarity of sight.
Your love is vast. The spell has been cast.
In the cauldron that will transform.

Susan Morgaine 2024

This is about my youngest, my beautiful son. He is in his thirties and for the past seven years has been held tight in the grip of severe mental illness. After several hospitalizations, therapists, programs, I have come to the conclusion that there will be no healing for him any time soon. Clinicians don't seem to really care; hospital personnel appear to just want him released. It does not matter that I beg them to not release him, it is done anyway.

After the last hospitalization release, it occurred to me that this is what his life will be like. He most likely will never be truly happy. I, too, as his mother, will help him through this as best I can for the rest of my life.

I am unable to change him; this work must be done by him, mentally, emotionally and spiritually. But I asked myself, what can *I* do? I have spent time with him in numerous hospitals, listened to him rant, rave, scream, yell for hours at a time. I have watched as he has sat in the dark so the electricity does not poison him, I have sat, cold, as he has shut off the heat because this, too, is poisoning him. I have taken him to emergency rooms time and again because of the things that are "being done" to him by person or persons unknown. He believes he is being radiated remotely or has had remote lobotomies by these same people. His father and I have been accused of being part of this cabal who want to kill him. He has assaulted his father in the past, and so I have sat in courtrooms explaining that these incidents are caused by severe mental illness, begging for him to not be thrown in jail.

So, what did I do? I turned to Ceridwen, for who better to understand the anguish of a mother who wishes to help her son.

We know from Her story the love she carried for both of her children, the bright, beautiful Creirwy and the dark Morfran. Morfran was also named Afagddu because of his supposed ugliness. Society, any society, is not kind to those they deem ugly or different.

Ceridwen worried about both of her children but knew, that because of her beauty, Creirwy's life would be easier, but Morfran? His life would be hard due to what others judged him to be.

Among other things, Ceridwen was a Goddess of magic and healing. She devised a means of extracting certain properties from healing herbs to give her beloved son the gifts of knowledge and wisdom, hoping this would counteract his outward ugliness.

To do this, she brought in Morda, a local blind man to keep the fire blazing under her large cauldron, getting a young boy, Gwion Bach, to stir her elixir constantly, allowing the herbs to infuse her potion. For one year and one day, Ceridwen traveled, coming back with this herb, this plant, this flower, until she had all that she needed. All that would be needed for Morfran was three drops, the rest would be poison. How unfortunate it is was that the potion was boiling and three drops flew out of the cauldron, landing on the hand of Gwion. He immediately brought his hand to his mouth, taking in the three drops meant for Morfran, from the mother who loved him so. The wisdom, the knowledge that should belong to Morfran, now belonged to Gwion Bach. Whether Gwion knew what he was doing or not, is up for debate.

Ceridwen felt the rage of a mother whose child is in pain. She pursued Gwion ferociously, through the incarnations of Hare/Greyhound, Salmon/Otter, Wren/Hawk and finally a grain of wheat, which was eaten by Ceridwen as Hen. Each of these animals has tremendous meaning within this mythology, relating to the elements, and our energy centers. All of these incarnations mean something within the realm of inner work, moving from Shadow to the higher self.

I have been undergoing changes in my physical and emotional worlds but some of the deepest work has been in the spiritual realm, applying myself to working with Shadow and healing to the best of my ability. I feel Ceridwen's rage. I feel her hurt. I feel her shattered heart.

It seems that starting this personal work eight years ago was to prepare me for the hardships that would start to beset my son only one year later.

In these years, I have struggled to understand the mental issues behind this, struggled to comprehend how and why this had happened to my baby boy. So, yes, I, too, have struggled, I have yelled, cried, watched him cry. I have been the one he turns to and, at present, I have been the one he has turned away from.

Ceridwen knows. Ceridwen supports. Ceridwen is there. I go to her and listen as she beckons me forward. I have looked into her Cauldron; I still look and will continue to look. With each look, transformation takes place within me.

I, seeking wisdom,
She, beckoning me forward.
Come, my daughter, come;
Into the depths, you will see—
All there is you need.
Face yourself, face your Shadow.
Grow strong in the wisdom you seek.

Susan Morgaine 2024

Did I gain wisdom? I do not know, but I have struggled to learn to accept what is, and understand that, with all of my love for my child, what I can do pales in what he himself needs to do. I have realized that *this* work lies with him.

I worry continuously but have stepped back, leaving our relationship in his hands. I reach out, say that I love him. I do not always get a response. I have tried and will continue to try. He knows I am there for him, as Morfran knew Ceridwen was there for him.

So, I wait for what the future will bring and continue to gain strength and wisdom from Ceridwen.

Mother Love

Reti Toriella

Brewing the Moon Child

Isaana B. Chrispin

In the cold, I held him—my gargoyle, my child,
That moon-face the world wouldn't touch.
I nursed him on secrets, on silent promises,
Stirred each hour into the cauldron's hush.

This love is a dark weight, soaked deep,
Heavy as rust blooming under the skin.
I forged him a shield, a cold armor, a skin of steel,
So even his grotesque form might find grace,
If only in the alchemy of shattered dreams.

Mothers are fools—I know this now—
We pour our hearts into blackened spells,
Wishing the world would gaze back softly,
See them as we see them: as saints, as sons.

Did I expect thanks when he drank?
Did I think the world would shift its gaze?
No. The potion spilled—its venom swallowed by another.
The cauldron boiled, scalding my hands,
As if even iron couldn't hold what I had forged.

I became something else:
A wolf with ribs like knives,
A hawk chasing shadows over bones,
A hunger with feathers and teeth.
Love burns, love watches, love transforms.

I wanted to swallow him whole, draw him back,
To unwind each mistake, clutch him from the world's bite.
But even mothers can't reclaim
What they've released.

We birth strangers,
Send them naked into the storm,
And we're left with this hollow cauldron,
The one they never tell you
Will always be empty,
The one they never tell you
You'll keep stirring,
Long after they're gone.

Cerridwen's Cauldron: Maternal Transformation through the Alchemy of Sacred Rage into Creative Expression

Maria Kefalogianni

Motherhood has been a tumultuous dance with my entire existence. With three beautiful children, my inward spiral journey through my births and initiations embody Cerridwen's three expressions: the Divine Mother with my first birth, the Dark Goddess during my second postpartum, and the Goddess of creation, poetic inspiration, and transformation, in my third pregnancy and post- birth.

Cerridwen is a powerful figure in Welsh mythology. She is regarded by many pagans as the Goddess of rebirth, inspiration and the keeper of the cauldron of knowledge. She is also known as a Goddess of poetic expression and prophecy. She supported me from a time unbeknown to me, as I'll show in my story.

Motherhood in my eyes is a mystical cauldron, much like Cerridwen's cauldron of knowledge. In our society, it is presented to be a serene and nurturing rite of passage. Balancing all roles required of us today feels like trying to walk on a celestial tightrope. Our breakdown is our making. Society shames our feelings of anger and rage. It conditions us to shut them down. This is a biproduct of indoctrinated patriarchal regimes, running through our own veins and bodies as women, daughters, and mothers.

When will we see this shutdown as a hangover from Eve's bite of the apple and her defiance in seeking the truth of our hearts? The structure of "motherhood" as we know it, is collapsing, giving rise to opportunities for our true wholeness.

My motherhood journey has been an invitation to alchemize deep ancestral and personal rage into transformation, creation, and poetic expression. I invite you, fellow mother, to join my ongoing inquiry: What if your motherly rage is the ultimate initiation, the clarion call of generations before you, urging you to inhabit and embody your fullness?

What if your rage is a dense rainfall from Grace, upon you, seeking to fulfil its mission through your expression, voice, and fiercely loving heart? In this ongoing inquiry, I have un-become in ways unfathomable to me. In my total breaking, I have been made.

Through surrendering to my third unplanned pregnancy, the myth of perfection shattered. Toko-pa Turner writes, this perfectionism is a great pillar of patriarchy "used to stem the rise of the wild feminine". Sacred rage, for me, constitutes, the holy grail. A process of conscious divination of seeding us back into our inherent blossoming. It is the medicine stirred by Cerridwen's hands, through us, to un-root and re-root us back into our fullness and expression of our truth. It is her invitation to radically accept our imperfections and embrace this surge of sacred medicine as the fuel for our transformation. Cerridwen's cauldron is often associated with the womb of creation and rebirth. She is depicted as a wise mother and a sorceress. After my third baby, my body became her cosmic cauldron. In this undoing, I became the finger, and she, the eternal palm. Upon her will, I have been stirred into old-new truths. Her magical brew was reignited and poured into my cells, where ancient wisdom spoke, and creative expression, poured out.

True transformations for us as mothers arrive after being literally "stirred" up, walking through the fire of the cauldron, the heat, and the wilful courageous walk through the shadows. This is one reason she is also considered, a Dark Goddess, misunderstood by many. Her story shows us that no Goddess is perfect. She alerts us to the potency of the potions made in her cauldron. If not cooked to the right temperature, or if the potion is given to the wrong people at the wrong time, it holds consequences. Yet, she also shows us that a goddess like Cerridwen holds the potency to meet any challenges presented her way.

As a young girl, I was well-versed in expression of anger. This energy came in waves of passion and intensity, too dense for my family to hold. It has been both the gift of my rebirth and my self-poison. It attached to me labelling and shaming, which I continue to decode and rewrite from my cellular memories, through ongoing self-mothering. Looking back, it was my embodied knowing of the injustice and grief of separation from our inner divinity—a dimension I was in touch with from an early age.

Life brought me to the UK in 2007 to train as a psychotherapist, where I learned to 'tame' this energy under a thinner veil of compassion. This veil, however, further buried my sacred rage in shame, so I could fit into UK culture. My psyche split deepened. This resurrected rage revealed itself again during my third postpartum period. On a rainy morning in 2023, I was sitting on my sofa, listening to a male spiritual guru while breastfeeding my third child. Drained, with black eyes from relentless lack of sleep, I felt engulfed in my motherhood journey without family support, nourishing three children, and trying to fulfill all the roles society asks of a woman, whilst navigating a spiritual awakening.

Suddenly, I felt an electrifying fire running through my body. It was deeply clarifying. I rose from my seat and stood in the truth of my voice. "No fucking guru talks about motherhood as a portal to spiritual awakening". I free fell into the potency of this energetic life force that reverence of rage gifted me. The moment felt like Cerridwen's transformative potion, stirring deeper layers of clarity for my story and the stories of women before me. For the first time, I saw in this outer expression, shame wasn't present; it had melted in the Goddess's Cauldron, in the heat of her fire all along my mothering journey.

From that point onwards, a fierce curiosity arose to consciously work with this potent energy, rather than perpetuating a self-pathology that keeps me and my ancestor's hostage to unspoken truths. Anger usually masks our sorrows and shame, but rage is a deep, heart-wrenching grief. It resurrected in me a primordial, guttural howling at the grief of all separation. I saw with clarity that my struggles with anger since childhood were divine gifts. Anchoring in the wisdom of the Goddess, I resurrected the embodied knowing that I stood on the shoulders of my ancestors. This energy called to be poured out, giving voice to the unvoiced and unspoken.

Cerridwen's name, though unknown to me by name until that point, was familiar in her mystery, potency, and sacred transforming powers, through my inner journey with the shadows. She had visited me before in shamanic journeys I had taken during motherhood, appearing as an old lady with white hair and black clothes, stirring a pot. Meeting her in visions I had, I was filled with awe and mystery, and at the time, fear. Looking back, my acquaintance with her was long forged, stretching back to my teenage years when she whispered and gifted me her prophetic abilities. "You will die in your mid-thirties," she said. Her prophecy never scared me. Standing by her wise company, I had a deep knowing merged with hers. Indeed, in my mid-thirties, an unplanned and profound awakening occurred, and the me I knew died.

Through my second pregnancy, my shell totally broke. This period marked a descent into the Goddess, as deep dark matter of my psyche rose to the surface to transmute, transform, and begin to reform into the alchemizing potion she beckoned me with. It was during covid. I was pregnant and suicidal; stripped naked into my bare being. Manifesting through my cosmic womb, which isn't separate from hers, I recall a deep dark night of the soul coinciding with a diagnosis of my neurodivergence. It was a time of a deeper call to my authentic being. I vividly recall Cerridwen's voice in one of these days: *"This is not you; this is clearing you from the inside, simply trus*t".

Existence was gifting me both physically and symbolically with rebirth and transformation, that Cerridwen is known for. She held my hand as she always had since I was little. Awakening to this voice solidified in this descent. Thanks to the inner clarity that had pre-existed, I had come to increasingly trust her faithful presence. As a Dark Goddess with prophetic abilities, she is feared by many.

After the surrender of the unplanned baby number three, Cerridwen began awakening even more potent powers of creation within me. As a mother tapping into deep and holy sacred rage, I began transmuting in my inner cauldron, alchemizing energies long forgotten, denied, and suppressed both within me and on behalf of women before me. The unspoken grief and rage were palpable. Dreams of ancestors kept coming in during this phase revealing that I was never alone. This knowing cut through any sense of isolation and separation. Memories and synchronicities begun to spontaneously emerge, showing me how a Goddess energy supported me and called me deeper into her potency.

I was being weaved into a tapestry unbeknown to my logical linear brain. Being the only woman from my extended family to go abroad for my studies, I soon realized this was a chosen mission. I was now called to lean in consciously. Originating from Crete, a deeply patriarchal island in Greece, I am a descendant of women in black clothes, hardworking women of service, women of deep sacred duty to give themselves in service for their families. My ancestors would self-sacrifice for their children at the cost of their own self-care, mental health, and at times, their lives. Through their heart of service, they forgot parts of themselves. Crucified on the cross of their self-abandonment, they endured disrespect. This regime holds deep in my bodily veins, that I am still shedding layers from within.

Rage was my untangling force. It pierced the thick veil of ignorance, unveiling ancestral grief for my own story and the women before me, at once. It gifted me sharp clarity for sharp boundaries, a rebellious ring-fencing of MY time, and devoting time, for once, to my whole self and creative expression. Love and grief began pouring in for my ancestral lineage—their hardships, struggles, service, and divine spirit. During the pit of motherhood, Cerridwen supported me in deepening my surrender to her energy and fire. Eight years ago, while pregnant with my first son, I had a prophetic dream of spitting butterflies. This dream made sense when poetry began to pour into me this time round. In the depths of holy rage, the fire of creation birthed me anew through recycled rhymes of my burnt ashes. Poetry arrived amid changing nappies, with an energy that bathed me in goosebumps. I would receive a poem title, and all activity would cease to capture this inspiration. Poems arrived unpolished, untethered, raw, and complete with a compelling force of light and truth. It felt like a fusion of spirit with human, serving a sacred purpose. They were alchemical potions, asking me to release and let go the shackles of patriarchy, self-abandonment, and the stories and beliefs of powerlessness passed down through lifetimes and generations. My logical left brain had no power left to lead in the rational way it once did. My body was in the lead. I had spent my whole life in the grail of holy rage, but it was never used or called for conscious inspiration until this time in my life.

In the mycelium of my veins, amidst motherhood dreams, I saw, felt, and held space for it all. I was invited to radical mothering, weaving my core wounds into my inner belonging. There were days I travelled through different timelines within my body. I could smell my grandmother's home, or I was transported into what felt like memories of the future. I meticulously gathered all the stories of women in my lineage—beaten, abused, attempting to kill themselves, women who lost babies and children at war or from ill health. These stories resurrected within me, carried down the ancestral body. I was homing it all.

At times, my trust was shaken, and doubt crept in. Cerridwen invited all these emotions as medicinal remedies for her magical potion. She whispered to me to look with the eyes of her creation, to see the wisdom hidden within the daily chores of motherhood.

When my body would fall into a slumber, a kind of protest, against all chores laid on my shoulders, I'd call upon her help and seek her guidance. "*Show me what's to be seen*," I'd ask. My tears would pour through while washing the dishes, knowing deeply these were tears watering old, abandoned olive yards within me. Surges of sacred rage would arise in the middle of my day, cutting through me for the injustice, death, and oblivion of our sacredness as divine mothers.

Grief was composting in my body. Humans possess an unimaginable amount of will and power. Even goddesses struggle sometimes, yet those are moments of holy divination. In her cosmic brew, Cerridwen gifted me new insights about parenting. She has shown me what becoming fiercely loving to my children truly meant. She gifted me a newfound capacity to implement boundaries that were previously blurred and buried behind ancient ruins of confused love and inconsistent holding. Untangling from co-dependent dynamics was another gift. She taught me what it means to move away from a power over paradigm, that kept my heart caged for so long.

By working consciously with her energy, I entered deeper realms and realities, fueling me with an influx of synchronicities and miracles in my daily life. As one of the five goddesses of Avalon, she is the guardian of spiritual transformation and the dispenser of righteous counsel and ultimate justice. I created three communities upon this journey and started three books. Cerridwen warns us that that burying her light is no longer an option. Calling in our tribe around the cauldron, is her invitation.

Cerridwen's cauldron, a symbol of profound alchemy, teaches us that our bodies are vessels of immense power and potential. As mothers, we carry the wisdom of our ancestors and the strength of our lineage within us. By acknowledging and honouring our sacred rage, we break free from the chains of patriarchal conditioning and step into our true wholeness. Waking up to our rage is waking up from our indoctrinated apathy (Cole, 2023). Though it was granted as our poison, it also is our antidote (Chemaly, 2019). Cerridwen encourages us to keep the faith blindly in this infinite inspiration and to follow the recipe of the potion, to mature in us. It invites us to draw the courage and drink from our own cup of life. To be able to do that we must resurrect all crucified parts of our soul, body, and mind, tied to the chains of the past. We need a tribe to break the loneliness of this un-ravelling. She points to us to be who we are, divine vessels of imperfection. A messy and poignant dereliction of dark and light. This journey is not about perfection. If you are a mother that seeks to liberate herself from the dynasty of more, then you are not alone. Open your palms and receive her wisdom. Cerridwen will prepare your transformation potion, but it is down to your human hands to be drunk in it.

BIBLIOGRAPHY:

Toko-pa Turner (2017). *Belonging: Remembering Ourselves Home*. Her Own Room Press.

Chemaly, Soraya. (2019). *Rage Becomes Her: The power of Women's anger. Atria.*

Riley, Cole Arthur. Black Liturgies. Facebook post November 11, 2023.

Cerridwen Prayer

Molly Remer

Goddess of the wild earth
sweep me up into your
forest cauldron.
Let my buried shame and sadness
rise into steam and drift away.
Stir me into stone and vine
twine canes of raspberries
around my shoulders
and streak my face
and fingertips
with the red juices
of wildberry worship.
Sink the blackbird's song
into my heart and
let my hopes rise high
on the wings of hawk.
Let your courage curl
into my ears
so that I might hear
my own mystery
being played on the wind and free my feet
that I may dance my truth into being
under a cathedral built of branches
and blue sky.
Please grant me a tender moment
of sweet surprise
as I feel these fragments of magic
tickle my bones
back into life.

Embed this knowing
under my skin
that I might feel my pulse
beat in time
with your rhythms.
Thank you.

Originally published in: *Goddess Devotional: A Prayerbook Honoring the Sacred,* 2019.

Initiatrix: Goddess of Transformation

Reti Toriella

Mistress of the Cauldron

Erika Lopp

Myth will tell you little of my deeds. Many will find me wicked, being fed bits and pieces of my tale woven into infamous stories of hag-like witches stirring their alchemical brews. I AM NOT SHE. I am guardian to the grail, the sacred cauldron of truth with the power to transmute all who drink from it. My names are many: Dark Goddess, Lady of Shadows and Fate, and Cerridwen, Mistress of the Great Cauldron. I take on many guises for I am at my core a shapeshifter. I am pure inspiration! I will lead you on the painful journey to the cave of your soul where your truest self is hidden. The road to personal evolution is wrought with peril. Be brave and honest with yourself. Do not misunderstand my darkness for wickedness; that is not my aim. Nor is it my desire for you to find fault with your shadows, but rather to shed light upon them. My sacred charge is to brew the healing and transformative potion, Awen. I will share with you a sip, if you are courageous enough to partake. It is both bitter and sweet to the taste. I am that which brings about uncomfortable change, I dwell in the liminal awaiting your call.

But remember the wisdom I offer is not for the faint of heart. If you call for me, I will give chase. I will run down that which holds you back and uncover the pain within. DO NOT FEAR ME. Do not hate me for acting as your mirror. Revel in your flaws; they may reveal your strengths. The power to reflect one's shadows is a blessing and a curse. Long have I been reviled for my offerings, a dark mother who heals the spirit through painful truths. My gift is freedom to those who dare to know themselves completely. Step into your shadow and reveal the light within. Rebirth awaits!

Prayer to Cerridwen:

Cerridwen, Mistress of the cauldron of truth, brewer of the potion Awen, I ask for your aid. To drink from your enchanted brew brings knowledge of self and wisdom. Hold my hand as I delve into the uncomfortable memories of my past. Shed light on my shadows so that I may burn away that which blocks me from my truest path. I am a seeker of transformative wisdom. With reverence and respect, I honor you.

The Howling Moon

Katie Daly (age 10)

When I am playing magical games, I love having the power to shapeshift into a wolf. Being a wolf reminds me of my nanny Cathy because her last name was Phelan, which is Faolán in Irish. This translates as Little Wolf. That means my ancestors were wolf hunters, wolf breeders, or wolf tamers. They could possibly even be descendants of werewolves!

Potion for a New Day

Jeanine Otte

After the Prayer of St. Francis

Dear Cerridwen,
Make me a Potion of Self Desire
Arouse power in my heart
Compassion to my nerves
Rest my bones

Make me an Instrument of My Calling
Born of Mothers 'Songs
And Trees 'Delight
Of Childhood Play
Imagination Infinite

Cerridwen, Dear Cerridwen,
Stir in Me the Gift Most Precious
Rose of Red Burn Passion
Of Love of Self
Of Grace Abundant

Swell in dark and light waters
Where vision beyond eyes sees
The Beauty
The Colors
The Wholeness
Of Me

Goddess Cerridwen

Terence Estrada

The Witch's Cauldron, Ceridwen's Oud

Kelly Murphy

Just the sight of a cauldron invokes the modern woman's inner witch, cue the potion's percolating sounds to awaken the enchantress within.

Her shelves are filled to the brim with glass jars topped with Snake Skins, Styrax, and rich Resins — it all begins and ends here. She can brew rituals capable of changing the course of history and health, manifesting destiny, peace, protection, and prosperity.

This is not a mystery. She can craft and curate potions for every affliction. The chains to resist this notion once locked tightly around her mind, now busted wide open.

It's just a fantasy, they say, yet she can conjure her powers and fields full of warriors by adding Black Hollyhock, Mandrake Root, and Hibiscus to her pot.

It can be a majestic massive cauldron, bold and beautiful — it can also be a kitchen bowl, leftover candle holder, cup, or a rock with a deep enough divot. She doesn't obsess, she uses what she has to create concoctions that evoke and imbibe the elixir. Her truest power lives and breathes in her intent.

She brings Sandalwood, and Tobacco Vanilla with a hint of something unique just to her. She churns her inner magic into her potion with her thoughts, chants, and spells. She dashes a dose of Obsidian, Mugwort, Juniper Berries, and Crow Skull Charms.

She summons an oud of rare Resins to raise the vibrations in her space, take dominion over her domain, or simply to inspire a tribal dance. Her heartstrings lead her to light a flame to bring sparks to her brew and the potency of purification and swift resolution. She stirs the pot of ultimate devotion to the dark goddess with Ocean Air, Labdanum Liquid Resin, Copal, Benzoin, and Dragon's Blood. She stops to inhale it all in for as long as it takes to supercharge her spirit.

This cauldron does not deliver a docile cry, but one of action, cupboards flying ajar as quickly as her ideas. Wafting throughout the space is an irresistible trance dripping with Amber and Apple, atop Cascarilla Wishing Powder and Blue Lotus. She thrusts out her book of shadows, keeping a record of the spells and mixtures that have wrought inexplicable change, swiftly, throughout her history and lineage – knowing well that she will pass this book onward to her descendants.

She trails Black Sand on the path, packing Seashells full of Rubies, raw Emerald stone, Larimar, and Tiger's Eye.

She knows she is safely surrounded by an unbreakable shield enabling her greatest powers to come rushing out. She doesn't hesitate and allows them to rise up out of the potion she puts in her pot — inviting her tarot deck, and ancient boards to the cosmic brew.

Snapdragons and Hawthorn Thorns, Iron Nails and Horned Gods, Blood Magic, and Devil's Heads, burning a Bay Leaf into her cauldron, the wish is granted before the smoke and ash vanish.

She is you. You are Her.

Cerridwen calls on us to return to the powers of our ancient selves — to remember we are born masters of the natural world. Within both live the keys to all magic and all possibilities.

Meet Me at the Cauldron.

Goddess Ground Down to Connect In

Sannie Cuddihy

Cauldron Womb

Sannie Cuddihy

I am a mother

I am a Goddess

Glowing inside and out

I hold life within my cauldron womb

A new generation of Goddess

My daughter

The future.

Cauldron Womb

Sannie Cuddihy

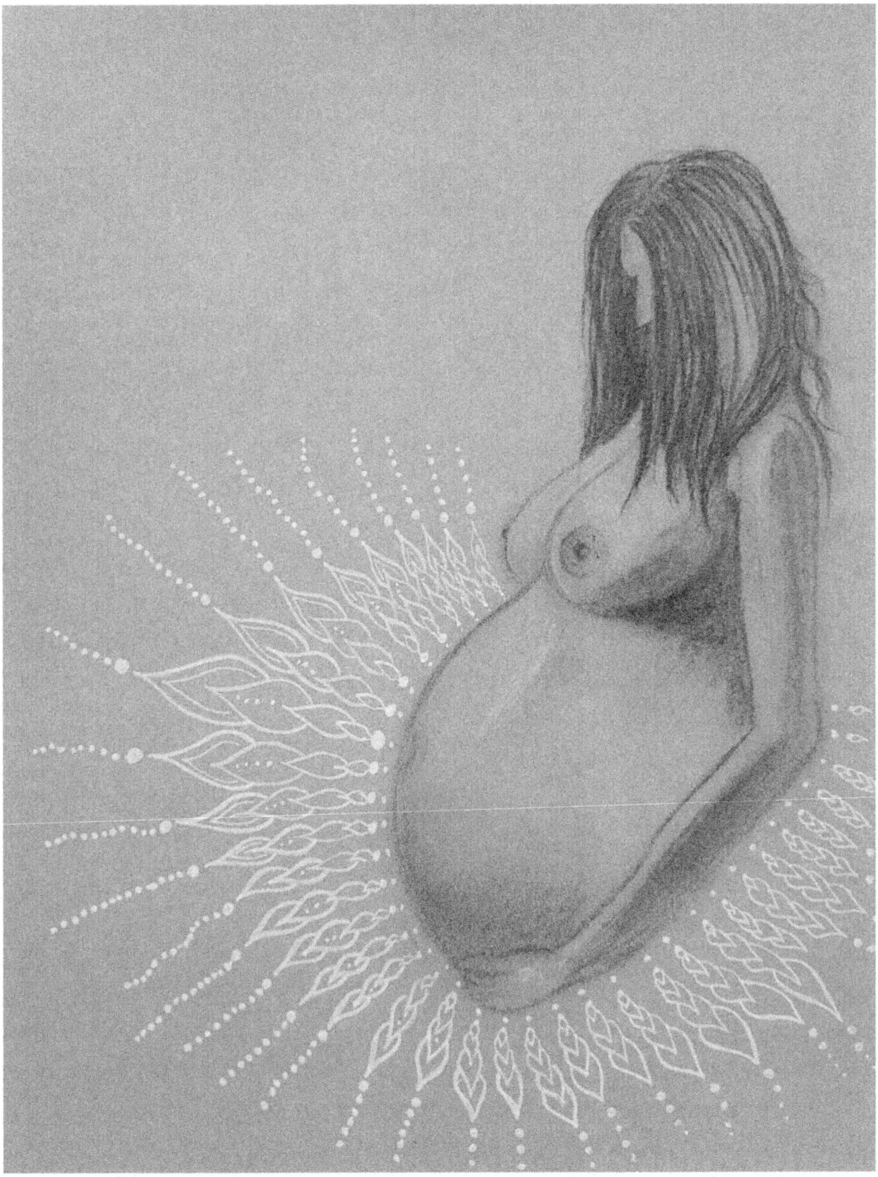

Simmering Beneath the Surface Seven Cauldrons:

Inspired by Cerridwen's Cauldron of Poetic Inspiration, Rebirth, Transformation and Medicinal Wisdom

Claire Dorey

The Cauldron of Bliss

In this cauldron she drowns in she is: a mermaid in a fishbowl; the Lady in the Lake; Morgen in the sea of Avalon; Delphine in her bathtub; Ophelia in a lily pond; a 'witch' on a ducking stool; a swirl of a girl caught in a maelstrom. Vortex sucking her down, a young life vanishing down a plughole, disorientated and gasping, she stops clawing at the water when her lungs become waterlogged. This experience is not entirely unpleasant. She's entered the blissful stage of drowning – acceptance and solitude. Floating peacefully in the aqua deep, skin flashing like fish scales, moving in ever slowing circles, in liquid trance, she's watching sunshine flood the water.

Death becomes a destination, with lifetimes of wisdom bubbling to the surface, as the Earth, a luminous pearl, slips beyond reach into the cold void of the cosmos.

They want to baptise this Pagan. Break her. Immersion. Asphyxiation. Out-of-body experience. Euphoria. Rebirth. Submission to the patriarch. Path of the sword.

Yet death by drowning wasn't to be her destiny. A leathery fist, with a righteous manicure (cleanliness is purity), tunic sleeves rolled up, is pulling her up out of the water, like an oyster from the seabed. As breath returns in a violent, lung splitting gasp, through a tangle of hair and sea foam, she focuses on a circle of godly faces peering down at her. She feels like Venus, reborn from the watery principles of "love" into "shame" and her first reaction is to cover herself.

The Cauldron of the Mothers

As I'm writing this it's occurring to me that biblical rebirth peels away the power of the birth mother and gives it to the patriarch, therefore I dedicate this cauldron to birth mothers and the ancestral wombs of the mother line. I'm hand building this earthenware pot myself, in my own image. I'm honouring meaning and wisdom, handed down by generations of artisans who coiled pots with breasts and buttocks; beaks and wings, legs and arms; spirals and spikes; spouts and horns.

I want to see what they saw, feel what they felt, up to their knees and elbows in red clay, birthing vessels, kneading life into ideas, layering coils, thumbing seams, thighs steadying ever-swelling form. Did they pour their dreams and expectations into the process like I am?

If the pots were daughters did the weight of clay and expectation barrel down on them as they bore the burden of this sort of love? Breaking bread, breaking pots, waters breaking. Let the mist carry away the burden of the water-carrier daughters.

Before I kiln fire my cauldron, sealing my own cooked-in conditioning into its structure, I'm putting it out in the clouds and mist for a day. Let the cold north wind blow through. Let the wind whistle across the top of the pot I put out to grass and play it like a pipe flute. Let the rain soak away sorrow and turn the unfired clay back to mud. This clay wants to return to Mother Earth. Let it all go. Today is for letting go. Tomorrow I shall build another.

The Cauldron of Dragon Ribs

This is the soot black, cast iron cauldron of sticks and stones and crumpled bones, in honour of children buried alive under rubble; in shallow or mass graves, whether victims of war, or victim to predators, many subject to cover ups, some found, some still in the ground.

Because child survivors build containers around life threatening experiences they may never speak about what happened to them. Disjointed memories; blank bits; stars glimpsed through a vent in the rubble; the sound of laughter as life continues for others out there in the sunshine; terror, pain, aloneness, flash, as if etched in celluloid, in fragile, fragmented greys, or in brutal, bloody, raw technicolour, on the screen of the dark subconscious that is oh so very hard to access through language.

Like these children, this cauldron can't remember how it came to be buried in the soil but it can remember how it feels being down there, forgotten, lost to the dust, amongst the dragon bones, waiting in silence.

Destroying dragons was a metaphor for destroying female energy and clearing the way for absolute male power, but why destroy the children? What can be said about the silencing of children at the hands of gibbering, cold-eyed, mad men, engorged and crazed by the pursuit of power?

I was going to write about Cerridwen's cauldron as a metaphor for the womb, umbilical cord reaching into the Underworld, seeking truth in dragon bones; the molten heart of Mother Earth spewing tides of red rage when she splits open; hissing cauldrons, fissures of steam and waking dragons breathing fire; kettles, as echo chambers, amplifying forgotten voices, simmering with visceral emotion about to blow; fury as a catalyst for change, but how can words describe the relentless perpetuation of patriarchal trauma creating a reality this bleak?

Survival rates for children growing up in matrilineal cultures are higher than patriarchal ones. I'm putting the patriarchal perpetuation of trauma into Cerridwen's cauldron to be transformed into witness-consciousness, compassion, protest. Let's sit with this for a while and decide what sort of world we want to live in, whilst the cold north wind blows through.

The Cauldron of the Holy Grail

When I was a wide-eyed child, blissfully reading fairytales, wondering why they had to kill the dragons, it was lost on me that dragons were a metaphor for female power and fairies were remnants of the Goddess, once exalted and answering to no man, now crushed and working for the patriarch.

Against a backdrop of medieval gender wars; religious wars (crusades); and horror and damnation, a plethora of male writers feverishly penned romantic fiction about righteous knights, living their best lives, in a world shaped by theories of female inferiority. Women were trophies (Guinevere, Maid Marion); female deities handed over their superpowers (Lady of the Lake); damsels were distressed and needed rescuing (Rapunzel, Sleeping Beauty); writers titillated by stripping proactive women to the bone (Lady Godiva); others were executed (Joan of Arc); unfaithful wives were beheaded or exiled (Marie/Genevieve of Brabant).

The frenzied hunt for the Holy Grail made men feel better about the destruction of divine female power, including the nurture that only matriarchal societies could give them which they desperately needed and yearned for.

They claim it is made of clay, metal, wood or stone. I say it is made of flesh. They say it might be somewhere in the holy land. I say it is right there in the holy belly of the woman sitting right next to you. The confusion surrounding the Holy Grail, symbol of spiritual wholeness and union with the divine, could have been resolved by reinstating the power of the mother, the wife, the Goddess, the uterus, the Wise Woman's cauldron, yet the "obvious" eluded these knights, who rushed across the world, escaping themselves, trying to plug the gaping hole in their own psyches.
Many scholars believe Cerridwen's poetic cauldron was the inspiration for the Holy Grail.

The Cauldron of Empirical Measurement

When the philosophy of 'medical science' was formalised, quantified and institutionalised, empirical evidence: observational and/or experimental became compulsory. It went like this: hypothesis; method; experiment; standardised apparatus; result reproduction; peer review; presentation; validation; acceptance.

Chrysanthemum. Mullein. Motherwort. Sage. How can a healer's fingers digging into the soil and seasons be empirically measured? How can Wise Women's innate wisdom; intuition; intention; sensory perception; aptitude for spell craft; psychic ability; connection to spirit, and capacity for love, compassion and dedication be empirically quantified?

Yarrow. Spikenard. Wormwood. Mint. Intuitive brewing is an essential, sensory and divine experience, steeped in generational knowing: when to add, when to refrain, how long to simmer, when to stir. Comfrey. Borage. Nettle. Henbane. Wise Woman herb craft was an age old, inherent and inherited practice, this vast knowledge held in the mind space, not written down: when to pick, where to forage, how to store, when to plant roots and seeds for next year's medicines.

Dittany. Hemlock. Mugwort. Pennyroyal. Balancing ingredients and dosage is a holistic art. The healer holds the power. Plants heal. Plants kill. In micro doses certain plants heal, in 'overdoses' they may be fatal. Herbs in Cerridwen's cauldron were boiled for a year and a day. The first three drops of potion gave the recipient oracular wisdom, the remaining liquid turned into poison.

Tansy. White Hellebore. Feverfew. Rue. The Middle Ages were a hostile time for women. The house of God maligned and distrusted female power. Enchanted infusions were eyed with suspicion. Possessors of "the uterus" had one purpose: to be vessels for breeding. Regulating the womb with drinkable magic (botanical emmenagogues and abortifacients); and woman's mysteries, including midwifery, were seen as dark arts and the domain of witches, somehow linked to voracious sexuality and copulating with the devil.

Astride science and magic, Wise Women and their cauldrons were pushed out of medicine.

In various legends, the character Morgan Le Fay, swung from compassionate to malicious; from divine to demonic; from supernatural healer to evil sorceress and adulterous seductress, illustrating wavering medieval attitudes towards Wise Woman healers.

The Cauldron of the Stars

It is midnight and I've been out in the woods with my Cosmic Spoon. This spoon is a metaphor for the cosmos in motion. I'm letting the motion of the night sky stir a mighty vat of botanics and moon water. Simmering away beneath the stars, silvery liquid slopping over the brim, this concoction is absorbing star energy. I'm breathing in the aroma of stars, waiting for miracles.

The philosophy of ancient medicine embodied astronomy and astrology. Twinkling stars, orbiting planets, the sun's path, comets, eclipses, moon phases, constellations of the zodiac and cosmic alignments were believed to affect body and psycho-spiritual well-being, so of course the cosmic was entwined in healing.

The asterism of Ursa Major, spinning round the North Star, is depicted on Samarra pottery as both a celestial dragon motif and as images of seraphic women with flowing hair, both forming the four 'directions' of the Swastika. Before it was corrupted this was a rapturously divine symbol, describing the motion of the matriverse, the cosmic womb space, a mighty orb, containing us all.

Many Celtic, Vedic, Far Eastern, Ancient Greek and Minoan pots and platters were decorated with the sacred Swastika. Perhaps this heavenly power symbol was an activator symbol, a spell not spoken, representing Ursa Major, the Cosmic Spoon, setting in motion the energy of whatever was incubating in, contained within, or served upon, the blessed vessel.

Of course, the direction of the divine Swastika was reversed by patriarchal 'forces,' who turned it into a symbol of destruction, even though trying to reverse the waves and currents of a cosmos in flow is as futile as Canute with his glad rags on, dragging his throne to the seashore, demanding the tempestuous tide stop at his toes.

It is midnight and I've been out in the woods searching for myself. Perhaps the missing ingredient in my own story is forgetting to look up. The love language of stars tells us all our experiences are as diverse as they are, yet it is in the dark in-between spaces that serenity, humility and healing can be found.

The Cauldron of the Poetic 3, 6 and 9

Poetic numbers underpin the structure of the universe: Psi, Phi, the Fibonacci Sequence, the Golden Spiral. In Goddess mythology the 'magnificent 3, 6, and 9,' thought by Tesla to be the keys to the secrets of matter and meaning, hold particular significance. Three is the Triple Goddess, the Three Matronae, the Triple Moon; Six is the Hexagon, which comes with a sting: beware the Hex (protect with the Pentacle). Six Vestal Virgins were keepers of the 'flame' (spark of creation). Nine is the number of months of human gestation; manifestations of the Goddess; realms of the World Tree; Muses; Mago; Sisters of Avalon. Multiplying any number with 369 gives the digital root 'nine'.

3,6 and 9 are encoded within Cerridwen's cauldron. Her brew was boiled for a year and a day, that's 366 days. Three drops of her potion gave the recipient oracular wisdom. Six herbs were added to the brew during a favourable astrological alignment. Nine maidens tended the fire below the cauldron.

Cerridwen's mighty, effervescing vat of botanicals transforms. I'm feeling lighter, just thinking about six pieces of baggage I could fling into it: anxiety, shame, self-doubt, dysfunctional demagogues, capitalism, the burden of being the water-carrier daughter.

Imagine being a plume of steam, spiralling above everyday troubles that ordinarily drag us down, which come to think about it, mainly centre around the theme of being female. In response I'm throwing three more pieces of baggage into the cauldron: the silencing of Wise Women Wisdom, eroding our sense of safety and connection to the healing paradise of the Goddess space, whether it be Eden or Avalon; man's inhumanity to women and children, and to all life including plants, animals and the Earth; the occupation of heaven and Earth by malign and warring patriarchal forces whose insurgent tentacles strangle our divine essence.

Peachy toes, stepping into public space, should not have to navigate everyday spaces as if they were war zones (of patriarchal making), ranging from perpetual micro aggressions such as catcalling, to bombing civilians.

In numerology the 3,6 and 9 are about manifestation. The Nine Sisters of Avalon practiced healing, herb craft, star watching, mathematics, music and shapeshifting. The Nine Muses were skilled in remembering, general knowledge, grace, poetry, astronomy, dance, music, in particular the flute, and the theatrical arts, including comedy. Creativity and connectivity are an energy exchange, raising all our vibration. Golden words and symbols, slipping off the tongue and spoon like medicine are love letters to life. Liquid poetry is far more effective than bellowing and mansplaining.

It seems to me, before we can know the secrets of the universe, we must know ourselves and that the answers lie in the wild, forgotten, magical in-between spaces we forget to inhabit. To ascend we must stir the cauldron. To ascend we must first descend into the underworld, deep into the belly of the dark subconscious.

Before we abandon ourselves to this perilous and necessary journey, let's listen to the cauldron singing to the sky in miracle tones, as the cold north wind blows through. Soon the clouds and mist will turn the unfired clay back into mud and it will return to Mother Earth. Today is for letting go. Tomorrow we'll build another.

A Breath of Inspiration

Rónán-Lukas Trodden

Prayer to Cerridwen

Arlene Bailey

Standing before Cerridwen's Cauldron
as it bubbles and churns, spewing
forth all manner of possibilities

Her ancient magic flowing forth
as both chaos and wisdom
intermingle, even as deceit
and theft hovers over it all

I can't help but wish...

If only we had this Enchantress and
Her magical cauldron in this now

If only we had Her wisdom and
determination to chase away
thievery and those that would
steal everything we've created

If only we had Her powers of
sorcery and transformation

Powers to see beyond the
deceit, lies and malice of
those who seek to dishonor
us and steal our magic

Sadly, I am not Cerridwen,
nor is any other woman
in this place and time

Even so, we may reach back to Her,
to our ancestors and their ways
of magic, wisdom, inspiration

Even in this now, the Cauldron
is still a woman's tool

Still a container filled with the
possibilities of all time

Still a container filled with the
magic of Awen surrounding
our hopes, dreams and
determination, all bubbling in
an elixir for this time and place

Still a vessel that holds the
deeply potent and sacred work
of banishing and destruction
of the evils of betrayal and malice,
thievery and forced upon ways
placed upon women of this time

Watching the fire burn and
the Cauldron bubble as we
embrace the power of flames
dancing in the ecstasy of
transformative birth,
we too are birthed anew
with both ancient magic
and ancestral wisdom

Magical Cerridwen!

Fearless Cerridwen!

Determined Cerridwen!

You who holds knowledge
of sorcery, enchantments
and gifts of prophesy,
create in us an inner cauldron
that holds both life and death,

both grief and elation,
a cauldron holding hope, love
and forgiveness, along with your
eternal elixir of transformation,
inspiration and right action

Blessed Cerridwen...

As women in this time
stand in the energies of
Air, Fire, Earth and Water,
may your cauldron of truth
and fires of transformation
shift swirl around us as
we banish the evils that
would enslave us and
create all things anew

As your sacred elixir fills us
with Awen and empowered
Wisdom of the Ages, may
the waters of birth and
renewal wrap around us,
as thievery and deceit
dissolve into brilliance
and reclamation of
each of our unique gifts

Submitting to both challenges
and transformation, may we
be gifted with knowledge
and renewal as we embrace
our personal magic and knowing

As the belly of our individual
cauldron holds all that we need,
offerings are placed on your altar
for inspiration, protection and
fearless determination in
the wake of the blatant,
embolden thievery of this time

May we know the words of magic
that are only for us and may
they spill forth as we conquer
those who would cheat us

May we embody the magic that
allows us with deep focus to
expand an image outward as
we embody the form we desire

Reaching deep within ourselves,
may we always seek transformation
especially in those times when others
would take what is rightfully ours

Walking with eyes wide open,
We bow to you Cerridwen, to
your magic and wisdom as we
embrace both the gifts and
uncertainties of this new now

May ancient Awen hold us

Cerridwen: Goddess of Inspiration and Wisdom

Pegi Eyers

Authorship, or She Writes the Story

Patricia Rose

Starry Mother, Goddess of Creation, Goddess of the Cauldron, Goddess of Inspiration – Stoke this soul fire; help me tend the flame of my own creative brew. May my Life's Soulful Expression be my Art. May all women find their voice. May all women own their inner magic.

Women are meant to birth many things ... we are mothers too much.

How this word – authorship – seeps into my Being and resonates like a great cavern, so much is in it: Make magic ... Stir the cauldron, boil the brew, spin the web, weave the tapestry, wield the words, fire the forge.

Authorship.

Isn't this what every woman secretly longs for? To be the author of her own life? To express from the soul? To *author* is to be an intentional creator. As Geppetto authored Pinocchio, as Louisa May Alcott authored *Little Women*, as Shakespeare authored *Hamlet*, as the Great Starry Mother authors the world.

How I want to clamor to the top of the mountain and yell to my sisters! Wake up from your trance! You are the toy maker! You are the stage director! We are lost in dreams ... under water, buffeted back and forth by waves, helpless, lost at sea ... slave to circumstance ... servants to the needs of others. We can turn the ship around! Come up from the dark depths where you sleep fitfully, come up to the helm, place your hands on the wheel. You are the captain and no other.

Authorship. We steer our sovereign ship. We allow loved ones on board inside the maternal hold ... they may travel with us by our caring consent, but not by our sacrifice, for it is a privilege to be held in the nurturing fold of women. This has been forgotten for too long, from the ages of our slavery and servitude ... a time which is not quite ended ... but will end soon ... because women are writing a new story.

I can feel the voice wanting to burst forth ... I can feel the voices of all women wanting to burst forth – in a growing rumble of thunder ... in a towering tidal wave breaking from the dam – that damn silencing ... that damn silencing of women for thousands of years. The dam cannot hold. I feel like a drop of water in that wave with all my sisters. Let us roll out on this titanic tide.

We write the story. Authorship!

Awen, An Invocation

Hayley Arrington

Many secrets are uncurled
From your mysterious brew's steam.
Many notions become unfurled
When we follow the winding stream.

But it all starts with a splash;
A splash on a finger.
And many are the secrets of holly, oak, and ash,
And many are the secrets that teasingly linger.

I ask for a taste--
One drop will make me full.
For from your cauldron
Comes inspiration.
The cauldron of Cerridwen:
Beautiful sights and Awen.

Cerridwen

Lisbeth Cheever-Gessaman

Retrieving the Black Rose: Dream Divination, Transformation, and Initiation with Cerridwen

Kay Louise Aldred

Dream Divination:

Last night I dreamt of searching for a necklace of protection.

In the box, I found a gold rosary with tiny solid yellow beads of gold and a black rose instead of a crucifix at the centre.

Transformation:

I deliberately chose to dress in a 'non-binary' way – and was leaving my childhood.

My mother was indifferent in the dream. An absent presence.

The patriarch of the dream – my father – gave me £20. He seemed pleased with himself about this. Jolly. But it felt conditional.

Initiation with Cerridwen and retrieval of the Black Rose:

Things are shifting. Pathologising our intuition, creativity, and internal ways of knowing – plus diminishing and undermining our internal spiritual authority – is no longer possible.

Cauldron Goddess Prayer

Molly Remer

Sweep me into the cauldron
as the first tendrils
of steam begin to rise.
Alert me to the bubbling within my chest
and to the taste of joy.
Guide me into the depths
where I might steep in my own knowing
and discover questions
I've forgotten how to ask
are waiting to be stirred up
from the bottom until
they become entwined with
a dash of destiny
and a scoop of power.
Stir me into the abyss of the unknown
where I might discover
whole worlds of possibility beneath my skin.
Soften me, tenderize me,
meld me into mellowness,
and spice my senses with awareness.
Let me brew into complexity, richness,
and depth,
as I drink deeply from my own life
and savor the flavor
in this cauldron of being,
becoming,
birthing,
and breathing.

Originally published in: *Goddess Devotional: A Prayerbook Honoring the Sacred*, 2019.

Moon Witch

Kat Shaw

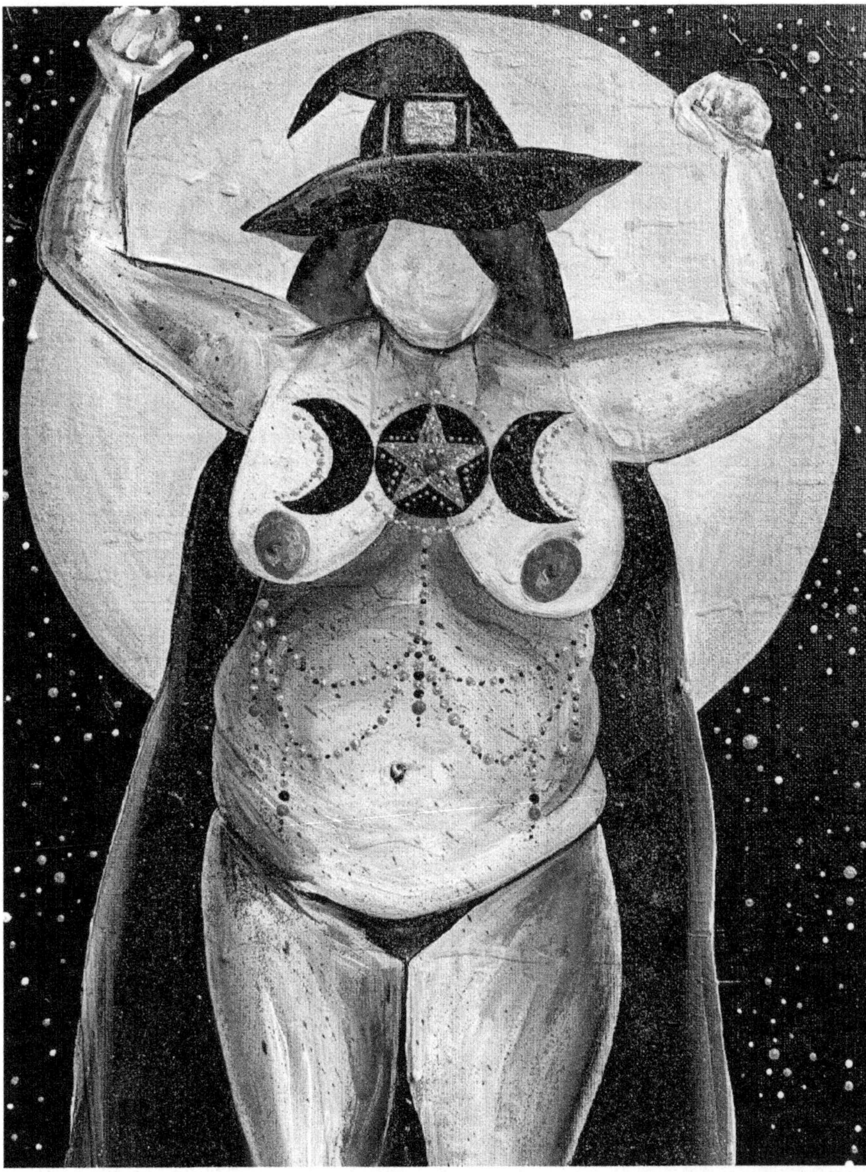

Mother – Stepmother – Friend

Sadie Laurenti-Whitley

In Cerridwen's mythical story the cauldron fractures, and the stream of poison flows out when the hopes and dreams of the potion that was stirred for a year and a day was suddenly changed. The three droplets of the potion splash up in the air and a droplet lands on Gwion's finger which he quickly licks. When Gwion licks the potion from his finger it changes everything that Cerridwen was hoping, dreaming and whispering in the cauldron for her son for that year and a day.

In my life story I witness the same hopes and dreams, and then the changes after that first year of my second marriage, and as a new stepmother to four children. The layers were inverted and the fractures appeared.

It's Friday. My established routine for Fridays is always a bit hectic. I am already feeling the stress as I fight traffic on my way home with a few stops on the way. On Fridays I leave work two hours earlier than the rest of my work week. The 405 freeway in California is slow and daunting with traffic. I slowly make my way to my neighborhood. I get home and change my clothes, and then I pick up the girls from Montessori school. My son is always home from school before I arrive.

Soon my husband will be in our driveway with his four kids. And so, it begins. The Friday night pizza preparation for nine people. It is always a very busy evening for me as I try my best to make pizza dough from scratch. The process of baking pizza is somewhat like this: all of the kids have different taste buds; likes and dislikes, everyone likes something different on their pizza. We begin with vegetarian pizza, meat pizza, sauce and cheese pizza, only sauce on the pizza or even an only cheese on the pizza request. At times it is [but yes] please add the mushrooms, and then, sometimes one of the kids will ask for a plain pizza dough baked with no toppings. I do love preparing fresh pizza dough, and everyone seems to enjoy it. This is where I lick my finger and draw a number 1 in the air. I got this.

I always knew I wanted to be a mother. I always wanted a big family like the Brady Bunch, an American sitcom that is always filled with drama, comedy and lessons from all the characters with six children that are a stepfamily. A stepfamily in a Hollywood show is never the real-life story.

My mother was a single mother until I was twelve ¾ old. That ¾ means the world to me! I will always hold on to that ¾ as I loved being my mother's only daughter. I got so many kisses from her in my first twelve ¾ of my life. I still cherish those memories. Things changed when my mother married my stepfather. We became a stepfamily. He had two adult children, and my mother came with two kids, her son and myself. The kisses from my mother became infrequent as her own life changed as she drew her attention to her husband. We had a good life. Later in my adult life I learn the importance of being my husband's partner and honouring our marriage by witnessing how my mother brought her marriage together in a unified manner. It reminds me of a conductor of an orchestra who waves the baton to bring the music together. My mother was a lot like that.

I celebrated my twenty first birthday as a new mother to a son. Sadly, soon after my third child was born at age thirty, my marriage ended far too soon. My life quickly changed. I became a single mother. It was not what I had dreamt my life to be as a wife and mother.

I was able to provide my children with a sacred home that they can call their own. A safe place to play and be joyful. I played and loved on them often. I did all this whilst grieving the loss of my marriage. I tried not to show the kids my own emotions and sadness as they were young and needed me to be stable. The reality is that they knew I was sad. Kids know. Trying to hide my sadness didn't really work well, however, we got through those tough moments together.

Dating was not on my radar. The universe had other plans for me. You guessed it, the Brady Bunch Hollywood sitcom would become my own story years later.

I married my dream man. He has four children of his own which share time with both parents. The Brady Bunch sitcom had six kids; I managed to have my own Brady Bunch family plus one (seven). Score!

Pizza was always fulfilling to my soul. I always felt accomplished that I could make fresh dough and bake a delicious pizza. The toppings were always the stress point of the baking process as each kid would request different toppings. I still obliged and baked what they wanted on their pizza. Stay with me on this story because it was Friday pizza night when I went to pieces. This is where the layers compounded, soon to become inverted to the reality of being a perfectly imperfect stepfamily.

As the car lights illuminated the driveway, visible from the kitchen window, I would announce to my kids that dad and crew had arrived. Sometimes the girls ran to the door. My son would be behind them, or as any pre-teen would do, he stayed in his room until everyone walked in the door. Each Friday was different. Some were joyous and others were stressful.

I love being a mother to my children, and now, I've got four more from my husband's previous marriage. Being the stepmother was a whole new role that came without instructions. I knew marrying my dream man came with some different responsibilities and challenges piling on to those I already had in my life.

Welcome to my world of being a stepmother of two boys, and two girls. When our union became a blended family, my children were young and my husband's children were a bit older.

Two stepsons: One, ten-years-old with severe autism yet a heart full of love.

The second stepson is a teenager going through all the things young teen boys go through as well as figuring life after divorced parents. Having to share time between parents' homes is very difficult for him. Luckily, his school friends were mostly in our neighborhood as our home was not too far from his primary home with his mum. He loves music, surfing, and pizza. He was a teenage boy looking for acceptance just like I was in this family as the stepmother. We never spoke about our feelings or better yet, we did not know how to speak or ask for how we could support each other emotionally in this new family unit.

Two daughters: A teenager that was full of life, a bookworm. She loved crafts, which she learned from her mum.

The youngest of the two girls was 6 years old. The attention seeker full of talent. We obliged her efforts. She is cute as a button, and it's a delight to be in her company. She was always dancing and singing. Many times, my living room turned into a grandstand for her to sing and dance. I was her biggest fan.

Things became more challenging. A lot of different emotions, moods, exhaustion, feelings that were like a storm in the night without a warning. When that storm showed up, I didn't know when or from which direction it would come from. I was on high alert 100% of the time when my step kids came to visit our home from Friday through Sunday. After my first year as a stepmother, I decided to seek a counselor with experience in stepfamilies. I was seeking the "genie in the bottle," with all the answers, and the potion to make it all better. After eight months of counseling on my own, I asked my husband if he would join me because our marriage was starting to feel the stress. He did. We tried different strategies with the kids' visits to our home. I tried my best, yet sometimes I would become very annoyed by them for seeking all the attention from their dad and leaving me behind or excluding me. Were they really excluding me or was this what I imagined they were doing?

Our marriage was paramount to both of us. We engaged together to make peace. At first, I thought it would be easier to go our sperate ways. Then, the thought of not being with my husband would bring me an immense amount of sadness. Running away or giving up was not a choice for me as a mother, stepmother and wife.

I was not the disciplinary type of stepmother as it was not my place to be the disciplinarian, in my opinion. What I learned in counseling is to be a friend to my step kids rather than trying to be the stepmother. I never expected them to say I love you or to fill my heart like my own children did, however, they frequently filled my heart with joy and love when they were kind and caring. I loved that feeling. And sometimes I would be in full tears upset with my step kids for their unkind behaviours.

Pepperoni or no pepperoni. Cheese or no cheese, wait, was that orange cheese or white cheese, vegetables or no vegetables. Pineapples on pizza, I don't think so. The cheese on pizza became a fiasco. Literally. I decided that cheddar cheese on pizza was not what a pizza dough should have on it. I announced to the kids that there would only be mozzarella on the pizza as it is more traditional. Did I just hear someone crying because I decided I didn't want to have cheddar (what they called orange cheese) on the pizza.

Tears. It started out with one stepchild complaining, and then all of them complained that there was no more cheddar on the pizza. When I say all of them, I mean ALL 7 of them at the table. I couldn't handle the disappointment in them any longer so I brought back the cheddar to the selection of the toppings. Happy family now? Nope!

A local pizza chef suggested I should bake small personal pizzas. Brilliant, why did I not think of this before? It seems like a simple solution. My reply of gratitude and excitement was very noticeable. A simple solution. Here I insert licked finger and two scores in the air for me. So I thought.

I get to bake individual pizzas. Each kid chose their toppings and preferred cheese. The excitement they displayed as I mentioned I was baking individual pizzas was a happy moment. The kids helped set the table. This happiness and excitement did not last for very long. Drum roll please. Disastrous. One of my step kids had a full meltdown when I placed his pizza on the table in front of him. He was so upset that he pushed the pizza towards one of the kids, and stated that he couldn't eat this pizza because the toppings should be on top of the cheese not the cheese on top of the toppings. I offered to make another pizza, he answered no.

The cracks are now showing up. A very upset teenager had me in full blown tears. This is when the rifts opened as if they were the Grand Canyon. I stood up, excused myself and left the house and walked for miles. I was feeling hopeless. I did not know how I could survive being a stepmother because no matter what I did, it was not good enough. When I returned home my husband and the kids were done with dinner. They all managed to finish their pizzas. Whatever he said to them decreased the tension. Each of them thanked me for their personal pizzas. I decided personal pizzas were a win-win.

As the years passed and they became adults, I matured in age with a little more experience under my belt as a mother and stepmother. I realized that what we all wanted was to be accepted, to be considered and included in the family. We were not always friends; however, we have learned to use our voices to express our feelings. The relationship that I currently share with my stepchildren is a bonus- friendship. A bonus in my life that truly fills me up with joy. We are considerate of each other and respectful. To get to this point in our relationship took a lot of effort with dedicated time in counseling. Giving them all the opportunity to express their feelings without me taking things personally. I learned to open my heart with no expectations; just pure love present to receive their words fully. This made a difference in our relationships.

The Friday night pizza fiasco taught me many lessons. I didn't need to control and put so much effort into our pizza nights. I just needed to be more open to listening to the kid's personal feelings. I should have been more flexible and understanding. I should have brought more fun and laughter to our evenings rather than my stress. I added stress to these Friday nights by trying to create a perfect experience. Yet, life is not perfect, and I definitely was not practicing to be that conductor in the orchestra that brought all the harmony together.

Cerridwen had a plan for her potion; it was to be tended to and stirred for a year and a day. She probably checked on Gwion often to be sure that he was stirring gently and slowly. The rage that Cerridwen went through when Gwion received the drop on his finger is very clear to me as I experienced my own rage and changes. The chase in Her story was my learning lesson in life as I aged with wisdom, understanding, consideration. Witnessing the transition in my stepchildren into their adulthood as we have healed our relationships with respect and consideration. I now consider them as my bonus step-kids and my friends. My heart is full. I'm glad I chased the lessons. I am glad that I didn't give up on this family. I am grateful that Cerridwen let me see Her story as my own transition from mother, stepmother to adoring my bonus step-adult kids as friends.

Giving up was never a choice. I am grateful to have my big family and now I get to enjoy my bonus Grandchildren as well!

Cerridwen

Andrea Redmond

Cerridwen's Spell

Hayley Arrington

I have been a scent on the breeze,
A drop of dew on a blade of grass.
I have been the pollen and the bee.
I am the ninth wave of the sea.

I have been the toil and the ease,
A taste of cheer in a welcome glass.
I have been the acorn on the tree.
I am the ninth wave of the sea.

I have been the warmth and the freeze,
A hand on the brow when you pass.
I have been the prayer and the plea.
I am the ninth wave of the sea.

The tradition of ecstatic poetry in the Welsh Celtic tradition is exemplified by the "I am poems" of the Medieval period. The most famous of these is attributed to Taliesin, Cerridwen's magical son. In her quest to get back the potion of inspiration he unwittingly consumed, Cerridwen created both the potion and the magical boy who would wield it. Together, mother and son created the highest form of inspiration, divine ecstatic inspiration.

Taliesin is a mytho-historical figure who wrote praise poems for the king of Rheged as well as ecstatic I am poems. These ecstatic poems speak to a deep connection to nature and the Celtic Otherworld. Cerridwen is a mother and a witch. It is probably because of her being named witch that she has also been named crone, what popular culture calls "wicked witch." But Celtic myth loves a double and so Cerridwen being both mother to a newborn son and a crone over a roiling cauldron does not trouble anyone.

Cerridwen creates in the form of life and inspiration, that which is called Awen, and destroys, for example when the dross from the cauldron of inspiration became poison and when she sought to literally destroy the boy who would become Taliesin.

In my poem, I sought to show these dichotomies. Beyond the ninth wave is where the Otherworld lies. Cerridwen is a liminal figure. She is both a witch (a magical woman) and a Goddess. In the early tales, witches and faeries are very similar; they are both magical women. Cerridwen both bears the actual cauldron of inspiration where Awen was brewed and is herself this cauldron when she bore the great bard, Taliesin. Cerridwen is a magical woman who rules over liminal spaces. She lives at Lake Tegid. Lakes are often entrances to the Otherworld in Celtic myth. The Lake also acts as a mirror to her cauldron. She oversees both liminal places. She can go between these places. When you drink of the brew of the Otherworld, you receive divine inspiration, Awen. We who seek Awen seek the inspiration of the Otherworld. We seek to traverse the liminal spaces where divine inspiration reigns and where we can feel the guidance of Cerridwen and other Goddesses like her who both challenge and comfort.

Photo by Chelsea Arrington

Cerridwen Shrine

Chelsea Arrington

Spirals dance in my cauldron as I stir for a year
and a day. Stars swirl and ignite within and I sing
to keep time: a steady rhythm: a drum-beat
older than the sea, younger than morning's first dew.
My potion flows through millennia,
through crystal-topped mountains,
through sapphire and rubied galaxies, and remains
in my cauldron, as the spoon sways to my croon.
Circle round, again and again, spinning
through the clear waters of sooth and song.
Mine is the breath of Awen and I speak
only what is true. Come, drink of my pure
elixir. You need not seek it. My cauldron
is always within you.

Cauldron of Cerridwen Brew

Rebekah Myers

(DO NOT INGEST) ☠

Apple
Acorns (can be an irritant)
Ivy (can be an irritant)
Bay
Barley
Bergamot
Chamomile
Hazelnut
Sow's Thistle
Vervain
Honey
Almond Drops
Agate
Brown Jasper
Coral

Boil water in a cauldron over an open fire. Place ingredients into the cauldron.

Sit before it and be entranced by watching the flames. Breathe its mystic scent and invoke Cerridwen's wisdom.

DO NOT DRINK ☠

(Use Acorns and Ivy with caution.)

"Neud amug ynghadeir o beir Cerridwen!
Handid rydd fy nhafawd yn addawd gwawd Ogyrwen."

"Is not my chair protected by the cauldron of Cerridwen? Therefore, let my tongue be free in the sanctuary of the praise of the Goddess."

~ Taliesin, the Bard

The Cauldron of Cerridwen Visualization

C. Ara Campbell

The Great Cauldron of Cerridwen is a powerful gateway to magick, transformation and rebirth. Within it, great wisdom and mystery are revealed. Lay down in a comfortable place and take a few deep, centering breaths. Close your eyes if it is safe to do so and relax your body.

You find yourself on the shores of a beautiful island, the green trees swaying in the breeze. The waters that lick the shoreline are crystalline and seem to hum with some magical energy. The Moon is high in the sky, a perfect crescent pendant in the darkness. You walk up the hillside towards a clearing where a silver-haired woman stirs a great cauldron.

"My child, welcome. I am the Goddess Cerridwen, one of the ancient priestesses of this island of Avalon." she says. "Here within the sacred veil, all mysteries are known, for this is the birthplace of magick." She motioned to the great lake that glimmered in the distance. "Beyond the horizon, a mist gathers around this ancient isle, protecting it from eyes that do not have the sight to see Her great mystery. My Great Cauldron is the source of these mists filled with the waters of Avalon; they rise from my magick and protect this land. You are here because the ways are known to you, written on the marrow of your bones. You have come here seeking the guidance of the Great Cauldron, insight into the unseen."

Cerridwen motions for you to approach the cauldron and you move beside it staring into its depths. "The Cauldron is different things to different beings, and each one of us gleans a unique medicine from these waters. Come, stare into the depths. Seek the wisdom of what has brought you here. Do you desire answers? Clarity? Inspiration? Within the sacred waters, all things are possible. Ask the Cauldron and take the waters unto yourself."

You stare into the surface of the cauldron, which reflects back to you the moonlight overhead, your reflection and Cerridwen at your side. The water changes and you see images float across the surface, flowing from one into the next, a series of symbols and shapes that answer your inquiry. Take a few moments to allow the messages to flow to you. Cerridwen motions for you to scoop some of the water in your hand and drink. You follow her lead.

"The mystery of the Cauldron is known only to a few, and you have tasted of Her waters. They hold the magic of Avalon, the insight into all things. Take this knowledge with you when you go and follow the inspiration that it brings as it will flow into all aspects of your world."

Bring attention back to the body and slowly open your eyes, taking a few deep breaths. As you step back into your day, take the guidance and messages of Cerridwen with you.

Excerpt from *Dark Goddess Magick*, Fair Winds Press (2021).

The Cauldron

Julia Jeffries

Cerridwen: Alchemy and Flow

Kandice Mallinger

Goddess of the cauldron of transformation
Your initiation is the dark
The darkness is where I learn of death
Rebirth and creation
This life that I am blessed to live
Is the alchemical vessel – your cauldron
Which is stirred and tended with love
And ferocity by your watchful eye
Insight comes from heat
Simmering... for a time
Your time not mine
You pursue me relentlessly
Behind me yet with me
Fluid shapeshifting, flow
I am running through landscapes
Mind, body, spirit and time
Initiation is power
I find inspiration in the cauldron of life
I desire the wisdom of the Crone
Maiden and Mother I have been
And Crone transformation is near
Crone seeks me
Through time and space
Through many forms, many lives
Cerridwen, your alchemy opens my heart, prepares my mind
Rebirth arrives
And I realize the Crone is with me
Always
Wisdom flows from you
Crone Wisdom is my birthright
The culmination of life's journey; running, shapeshifting and transforming

Cerridwen, we are separate but one
You have gifted me with truth and insight
Goddess Cerridwen
My rebirth comes from traveling through the dark
Shapeshifting
Embracing creation
Alchemy and flow

I am Not the Same

Patricia Rose

I am in a no-man's land – an empty space that stretches into soft fog-like hues of grey. There is one Other with me, and we stand before a large fire pit in which a healthy bonfire glows and dances. I sense her behind me and off to my left. I am not called to turn and look ... She seems familiar. The blaze directly in front of me feels of more immediate importance. But in my peripheral vision I get a glimpse and a felt sense .... A robe of starlight ... a swirl and sparkle ... long moonlit hair ... the electric air of creative magic ... Guiding Presence .... Support.

In front of me, I see a brick ledge encircles the fire. The ledge is sitting height.

She – my Guide – is communicating clearly with me through the connection of our minds.

Step on to the ledge.

This will put me very close to the fire. I am wary; yet there is also an awareness it will be okay.

I step up as instructed and stand on the ledge – that fire ... crackling, snapping ... right there. I don't feel overwhelming heat. I'm safe, yet standing on the edge.

Above my head appears a cloudscape. I feel-sense what the clouds are .... I know. They are the things I want for myself in life ... my goals .... my dreams. They are just barely out of arm's length.

Reach.

Now I feel a little scared … and hesitate because I know what will happen. Every time I reach up, the fire will surge towards me and lick me. The knowing is there – I will ultimately be safe. But will I get burned? Will it hurt? I don't want to experience pain.

To reach the clouds – my goals and dreams – to even just touch them, I'm going to have to stretch … up on my toes, reaching all the way through my fingertips …

I reach …. And with a soft roar the fire lunges in my direction dousing me in flame. My alarm dissipates quickly into cautious curiosity as I experience heat, but no injury, no pain. Even so, it is very intimidating to have a bonfire lunge in one's direction.

Even in my stretching, I can't quite graze the clouds, let alone grasp at them.

Keep stretching.

I obey, trusting, and keep on … and begin to notice … I am changing … every time the fire licks me I am not what I was before. Goodness gracious! I am changing into the very essence of the goals and dreams just out of my grasp. . I am *metamorphosing* into *that* which I am reaching for.

And now I notice the clouds are also changing … and this is because I am changing! As I slowly morph … my goals and dreams shapeshift to match the new me. We are both in a state of shapeshifting.

And then a light bulb moment … an insight as to what is happening dawns on me …

It's all in the reaching. It doesn't matter that I never get my hands on those clouds – those goals.

It's in the reaching that alchemy happens. It's in the stretching you become what you seek.

The magic is in the stretching!

That sticky part of me that is too often mired in perfectionism is so relieved! Thank goodness! I don't have to actually "win" the goals?! My mind would have once perceived failure there – in that place where I missed the mark. But no, the progress occurs in the aiming! The transformation occurs in the going after it!

A new space opens inside of me .... A new freedom.

My analytical mind has to ask .... Do we ever catch up with the every-changing thing we're reaching for? Are we ever so transformed that the reaching ends? Do we find ourselves up with the clouds?

I sense a soft smile .... A chuckle perhaps ... I feel her wisdom forthcoming ...

Yes ... in a sense. It takes a lot of alchemy to change lead into gold.

I wonder at her meaning.

It can be done as I have done it. But that is another story – a misunderstood and misrepresented one. It has been told and retold by those who do not see clearly and the story has been distorted over time.

The culmination of true transformation results in the realization that you are all That – that which you have been seeking. You now embody it.

It is then that you are a true progenitor. It is then that you birth sacred creations into the world. You give back ... you author beauty and divinity and magic. You leave your mark ... you install art ... you set waves in motion that benefit humankind ... You have carved your name on Life.

I look her fully in the face now. She glimmers behind soft light. Will she disappear? She looks like she is smiling softly at some fond memory, her eyes far away. What is her legacy?

Who are you? I ask.

I am a Guide. I am the You of the future .... I am a You of the past. I am many possibilities. I am a pathway.
I am Further Ahead. Reach.

She is fading. All that surrounds me – the fire, the fog – is dissipating.

I wake. Wide-eyed ... new ... this new dawn lighting up my mind.

I am sprawled in my bed at home – not a misty place between worlds.

But I am not the same.

Cerridwen Cychwyn

Kate Greenwood

Cerridwen stirs Her cauldron,
steeping Her magical Brew,
Transformation,
Inspiration,
Deepest wisdom.

She turns my way,
veiled face,
asks me if I will taste.
If I will dare.
If I have the courage
of a heart strong and true.
'For the Cauldron boils not for cowards.'
And it is so much more than just a taste.
No tentative sip
that leaves room to
Change
One's
Mind.
There is only full immersion.

I choose to steep in Her cauldron,
to slough off the old patterns that keep us locked
in illusions of safety.
It's scary to be stripped down to the raw.
One would not be alone in choosing what
Looks
Like
Comfort.

But not for me!
I will take the dipper She offers me,
part my lips willingly,
with all my Sovereignty backing me,
and my Ancestors holding me.
I let Her tip the Brew into me.

Liquid black moonlight,
honeyed bitters,
fire of comet's flight.
Earthy as clay, as stone, as bone.
Coldest deepest water
tingling through me.
I become the Brew,
or it becomes me.
We ride throughout
all that is,
has ever been,
will ever be.
We are all and we are nothing.
No separation.

And when I come back to myself,
I am a different Self,
yet a truer Self.
At peace and in joy,
held with deepest love and compassion
in the arms of our Dark Mother,
Cerridwen Initiatrix.

Cauldron

Kat Shaw

Taking it to the Cauldron

Molly Remer

If I squint,
I can almost see steam lifting
from a cauldron in the forest
and smell change
drifting through the air.
I am looking at the shards
of the year,
some new-broken,
some re-collected,
some shining with possibility,
and I feel the call,
the urge,
the promise,
to tip them all into that bubbling vat
and see what She will steep me
into next.

Each year, in August, I honor what I call a "Cauldron Month" for myself. This is a month in which I "take it all to the cauldron" and let it bubble and brew and stew and percolate. I pull my energy further inward to let myself **listen** and **be** and to see what wants to emerge. It is a month in which I delete my social media apps and mindfully, intentionally draw my scattered attention inward in order to listen to my inner wisdom, to take all of my bubbling ideas to the metaphorical cauldron of my own being and see what is brewing, what is stewing, and what is ready to be dished up. I clarify goals for the remainder of the year, my next word of the year usually finds me, and I take time to consciously "steep" in my own flavor. It is a time of clarity and renewal for me, a time when I withdraw from outer life and re-collect my energy in order to determine where to put my focus for the remainder of the year.

It may seem strange to withdraw energetically at such a ripe and burgeoning time of the year, when life is bursting with things to harvest and ideas to share, but that is exactly why I do it. When life feels the most full, is when I know I most need some dedicated time of discernment. August, I find, is always a crucible of change and choice for me. It is when big projects are birthed, when new doors open, and when I reach metaphorical crossroads of change—crossroads in which I decide what to harvest, see what has withered, and come to understand what to sacrifice.

We are held between
summer's fatigue
and summer's fire,
there has been a blooming
and a ripening,
and now a harvesting and a fading,
as the time comes
to turn the page.

Cauldron Month dates back to 2016, a year in which my pace of living became unsustainable and I experienced a persistent and inexplicable cough that lasted for six full months. After this experience, I came to clearly see a pattern in myself, of speeding up and revving harder and harder through the spring and summer, until I reach an annual point of having taken on too much, in which I must make choices about what to let go of and what to pursue. It helps to know it, to name it, to say to myself: *oh, yes, this. Cauldron time is here again.* The understanding of this pattern has helped me to prepare for it, when I feel the familiar tension, the drive to push and speed, I step back instead. I sit down. I shut things off. I get still and I listen.

That first year, feeling overwhelmed by commitments and at my physical and temporal limits. I did a guided meditation called the Moon Goddess Ally Journey. During the meditation, in the temple in which I met the moon goddess, right as the meditation was coming to a close, the Cauldron from the *Womanrunes* oracle card system appeared quite clearly etched on the floor of the temple–it was very large, covering the whole floor, and felt like a dramatic and powerful wake-up call. I knew at this moment: *I need to take my life into the Cauldron. I need to see what is brewing. I need to steep in my own magic.* August has never been the same since.

Future Cauldron Months after having held varying experiences—some rich and powerful and some painful and challenging, what they all hold in common is that they illuminate the next steps and invite me into the next chapter. Some months, I've joked with friends have been "Slow Cooker Months" instead and some years—like 2020—have felt like Cauldron **Years**, in that the whole year is a process of transformation and re-emergence.

Each year, I do what I can to honor the call of the Cauldron—persistent and insistent—and in so doing I remember that it is often in the mess that the *story lives.* What sometimes bubbles up from the Cauldron during this period of incubation isn't particularly pretty, it can even be hard to confront, and yet, we continue to let it bubble, we continue to breathe and bear witness to our own interior lives, beyond the clamor and confusion of so many other voices that may fill our lives and days.

The Cauldron is a rune of alchemy and change, but also of centering of containment and contemplation—a marrying of what might seem like opposites, but that which really co-exist. During this month or another one that feels right to you (a lot of people choose December or January), consider taking it **all** to the metaphorical Cauldron of your life... what are you cooking? What flavors do you want to add? What do you want to create? What needs time and focus to bubble and brew? Can you allow yourself to steep in your own flavors? The Cauldron asks us what we're cooking, but it also offer boundaries, containment, a safe space in which to stew up our truest magic.

May you be inspired by some time in cauldron,
may you be inspired by time with yourself,
may you be inspired by that which surrounds you,
connected to Goddess,
connected to the earth,
connected to the animals, plants,
the wisdom of the wind,
the song of branches,
and the symphony
of river, stone,
leaf, and breath.

Take it to the Cauldron and listen to the deep within.

There are days when the sky
holds its breath
and dreams seep up
from the skin of the world
and into my feet.

A Prayer for Cauldron Time

Molly Remer

Startle me back to reality
on this land that I love
remembering my place
in the weeds and wind
flames sprouting from my shoulders
and roots springing from my toes.
Reborn each day beneath
a wide sky,
a cathedral of branches,
and a daily baptism
made of mud and stones.
Coax me into the cauldron
that I might steep in the stuff
of my own knowing,
savor the flavor
of my own mystery,
and stretch my fingers
into the singing recipe
of my own renewal.
Let me bite deeply
into the choicest portion
of my own life
and be nourished from within
wildly and well.

Originally published in: *Goddess Devotional: A Prayerbook Honoring the Sacred*, 2019.

Cerridwen

Arna Baartz

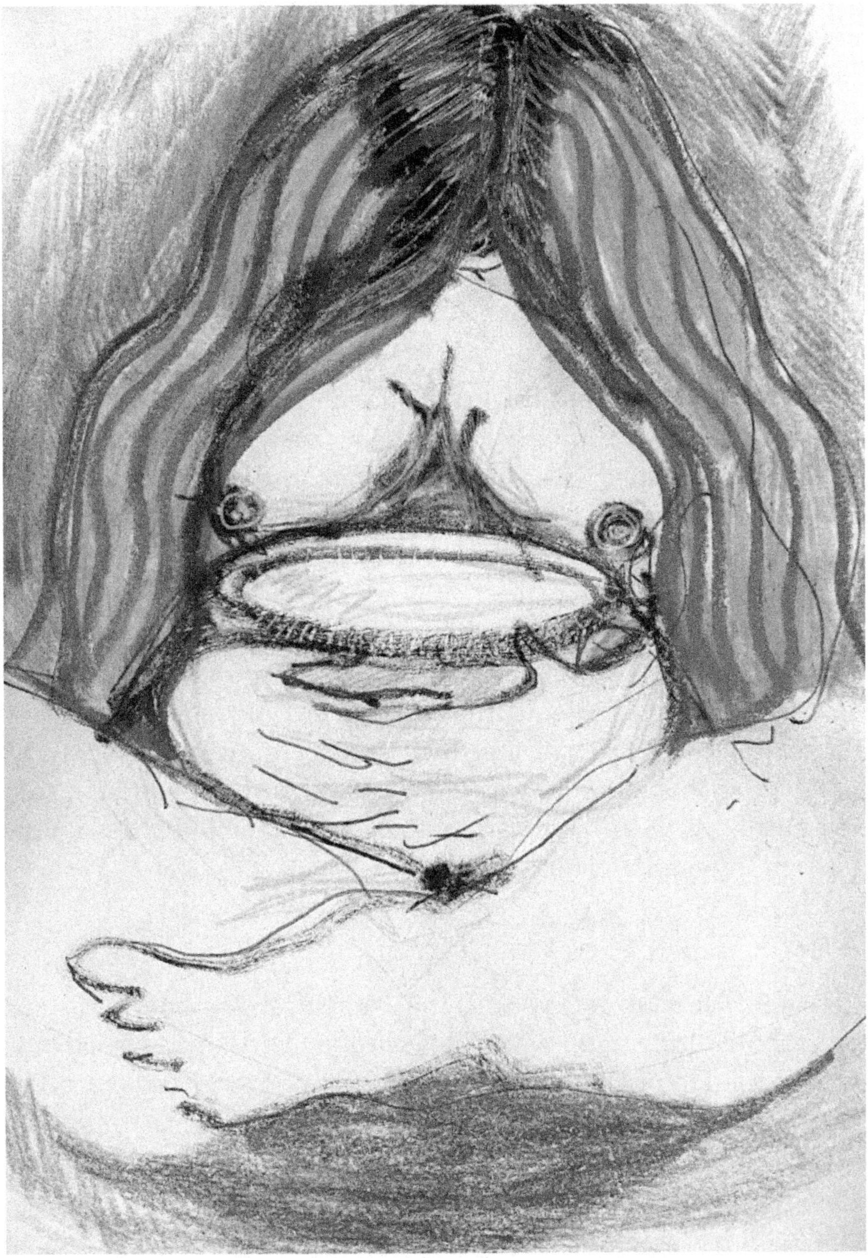

Cerridwen in the Woods

Alison Newvine

Cerridwen follow me
Cerridwen change with me
Til I dissolve in you
Cerridwen hunt for me
Cerridwen consume me
Til I be born through you

Cauldron

I went to the mountains to face my demons. The first time I'd gone there it had been summer and the days were beautiful. My little drum and I would go into the woods at sunrise to create sound. I'd unleash from within me the awe, gratitude, longing and some sadness too. Nights passed serenely with stars and crickets.

In the peace of life in these woods, I entered cauldron space. Something was brewing slowly within me from the sublime concoction of ingredients the woods provided. I was able to encounter the muse, to feel the sacred creative impulse throb within me. There was no pavement between my feet and the soft, red earth. My voice, so often self-censored and stifled, got a little taste of freedom and bliss.

Anger

Between summer and winter, the trappings of modern life had taken hold of me and I went back with my partner to his cabin in the wooded mountains to cleanse from it all. I had been struggling with confusion over which path I should take. I was frustrated that I kept going in circles, making the same mistakes, with my addiction to coffee and sugar. I was exhausted by swinging between confidence and insecurity. I expected the magic of the woods to smooth out the jaggedness of my angst and to provide easeful insight. I remembered how the muse had danced with my drum and me in the morning woods and I longed to meet her once more.

Of course, things did not go as planned.

I felt depressed, groggy and severely impatient with the hardships of a simple life. I tried to deal with my emotions. I kept up with my yoga practice, journaled, and exercised. I sawed wood, drank tea and rested. These actions helped to take the edge off, temporarily, but the edge would quickly return like a thin layer of dust on a shelf. The moment I had completely wiped it away, new specks would start to accumulate, making it harder to breathe, harder to see what was beneath the dust.

The cold was ruthless. I didn't drum. I didn't sing. I didn't talk about my brewing discontent. My voice felt even more constrained than it had back in the city.

One morning, after a particularly bad night's sleep, I awoke cold and bitter. I attempted to light the fire, irritated that warmth wasn't available at the press of a button. It would not light and I was getting frustrated. Anger at my own helplessness overcame me. I threw the matches against the wall, pulled on my boots and jacket, and ran out of the cabin towards the woods.

Below the surface frustration was a deeper rage that had been boiling in that cauldron. Rage at the theft of my sacred empowerment, stolen from me bit by bit by the Prince Charming narratives and Father God threats that created in me a belief in my inferiority, helplessness and desperate need to be saved.

Hare

It felt good to *run*, to move what my body was holding. The hut was still within my sightline when sharp pain in my heart stopped me in my tracks. I was still pulsating with fury that was about so much more than not lighting the fire.

I sat down on a rock and had a good cry. Or maybe it was a bad cry. I'd had a few of those over the past couple of days, the kind that goes on too long so that rather than purge the toxic emotion, the cry just exacerbates it and gives one a splitting headache and swollen face. Whichever kind of cry it was, it stopped when I saw something move in the brush a short distance away. The something was gray and about the size of a large rabbit. My attention was immediately refocused on this living being near me, a mammal, with red blood coursing through its veins just like mine, a being I had never met and would probably never encounter again. I began to really *look* at what was around me. Snow had fallen during the night, coating the branches of the trees. The skinny, spindly ones and the thick and sturdy ones were enfolded in glittering white dust. The snow was sparkling in the bits of sun that were peeking through the clouds. *This is amazing. It's absolutely beautiful and alive and every bit of it is conscious.*

After days feeling foggy minded, frustrated and lethargic, I was suddenly pulsating with energy. The woods had breathed life into me and I was delighted by all there was to see and feel. I felt soothed by this circle of wood, earth and snow around and beneath me. The soft, muted sun above me felt like the whisper of a kiss. My focus shifted from my own misery and was redirected out to the living, breathing woods and what it was telling me. Stories I knew I'd never be able to relay, wisdom I couldn't translate into words.

I looked back and saw the brown siding of the cabin peeking between the trees. A sisterhood of pine drew me further in, or maybe it was just one tree that caught my eye, or perhaps only a single branch, bent like a wise old woman's finger, beckoning me nearer. The next time I looked back towards where I'd come from, I couldn't see the hut anymore, nor could I pick out the brush where I'd seen the gray or white rabbit.

I set off in the direction I thought the cabin was hiding and looked for my footprints in the snow. That should be easy, just follow my footprints back the way I had come. When I tried to do this, the prints just led me in a circle back to the spot where I had discovered I was lost.

For a moment I thought I spotted the hut again, but I quickly saw that there were dead leaves peeking through trees. I realized what I had thought was the hut the last time I'd looked probably was not, and I was further away than I initially thought. I felt the panic that had been gathering around my edges suddenly go deep into my center, my head spinning violently, the sound of waves crashing in my ears. *I'm lost!*

Fish

It was as though the woods had swallowed me. My footprints had disappeared and I was drowning in the sea of snow. I had lost all sense of direction as though I were under water and not even sure which way was up.

I walked awhile and found myself in very unfamiliar terrain. Sitting down on a stump, the desire to just give up overtook me. I'd gone past the flesh and bone of hopelessness and I was into the marrow now, descending into the liquid core. *I don't know where I am. Who is going to help me? How will I ever get out?*

My tangible, physical situation had become an extension of the feelings I'd been swimming through for months. I'd felt trapped in my mental patterns and acceptable addictions. I'd felt *lost* for a while now and I'd been avoiding dealing with it. I was terrified to confront the massive uncertainty surrounding where my life was going, how I'd get there, if I'd be all right. Before I knew it, I'd forgotten my power to ***choose*** a path to walk. This emotional turmoil needed to find a much larger form or else I'd keep swimming around in the same small circles, decaying, rotting, forgetting. Losing my way forced me to look at how I was already drowning.

Bird

In addition to looming questions about career and higher education, things were not all fairytale roses and songbirds between my partner and me. I'd been feeling powerless in my life and this contributed to the persistent, irrational desire to have him take care of things for me. To *take care of me*. I felt like I needed him to make me speak when I couldn't (which, of course, he never would), to teach me everything I didn't know (which, of course, he never could) and, when it was too hard for me to learn things, to do them for me. This fantasy of a knight in shining armor, or prince with the castle in clouds, takes on many forms. It is also God in Heaven with his soaring white angels and his mighty judgment, deciding who will and will not be saved.

Sitting on the stump, there was a crow that flew back and forth over my head. I saw it but wasn't ready to listen to it. I wasn't ready to remember that I knew how to break the cage my psyche had manifested into physical reality and sprout my own wings.

Cold nibbled at my fingertips and toes so I began to walk. After about an hour and a half of wandering through the woods, I found a dirt road, covered in snow. I followed it down a steep incline and then stopped because I worried that I was getting further away from where the hut was. I turned around and went up the road instead.

When I got to the top of the road there was a fence and beyond that were railroad tracks. Technically, I was out of the woods, but I still had no idea where I was. I remembered that the railroad tracks by the fence were a frequent walk-to point from the cabin. I decided to walk along the fence and call out for my partner again, thinking that if he was still near home, and not off someplace else looking for me, then he would be able to hear me and come find me. I would periodically walk a short distance into the woods, keeping the fence in sight, to call out. I climbed a tree, trying to spot the hut from way up high but it was all branches, snow and dead leaves.

The shimmering black crow seemed to be following me this whole time, periodically cawing loudly, letting loose the frustration it must have felt in the face of my stubbornness. Then it was gone and I felt more alone than ever.

Grain

I walked along the fence for a while and then came to a point where it turned, and then kept going and going and going. I walked back to the road again, down a little ways, a little further than before, and then back up again, back to the fence, walking, calling, hoping I'd be found, fearing I would not. I'd decided against trying to get on the main road because the reality of backwoods men in pickup trucks was far more terrifying than whatever Mother Earth had hidden in her womb.

My voice started to loosen in the woods near that fence. Crying out again and again for a man to save me and hearing my voice echo that back revealed the bleeding wound of self-mistrust. The only way to begin to heal such a wound is to be thrown into a situation where you have to trust yourself in order to survive. To be completely swallowed by a reality bigger than the one you have created.

In a moment between bouts of franticness, determination and hopelessness, I felt myself crouching down to get close to the earth. So small in her vastness, I prayed to Her, to the Mother. I'd only begun praying to ***Her*** in recent years. The muscle was new, shaky. The prayer I repeated began, "Our Mother, who lives *within* us."

Incubation

Since childhood, whenever I was scared, I asked God to save me, even *after* I stopped believing in him. A reflex born of learned helplessness. This time it was not the Father Above but the Mother Within, whose presence I conjured. No Divine Force From Beyond, no God or prince or partner or even Goddess was going to rescue me. Even though I felt like I was entreating a loving, compassionate

Mother Goddess far beyond me, what I actually did was call upon ***my own power***, the power of the creative feminine within me, She Who Knows the Way.

Then I just screamed. Loudly. I screamed not to be found or even to be heard, but to let loose the anger, the childish frustration and remorse, to purge the deep, dark fear about my own survival. *Such fear.* It was human emotion unfiltered by reason or shame. Such pure emotion has enormous transformative power. Life let loose when I screamed and in that moment I was free.

My mind settled and opened. I remembered hearing about a dirt road leading to the neighbor's property and I tried to recall whether that road started at the fence. Suddenly, it seemed ridiculous not to at least *try* to take that road down as far as it would go and, if it led me nowhere, I could always come back to the fence. I had seen the neighbor's property the other day and noted the duo of trailers parked opposite a bright orange fireplace.

I began walking back down that snow covered road, retracing steps I'd taken dozens of times already this morning. This time I went past the point I'd gone before, went down down down the hill and started to see different trees, different piles of snow and sticks, a different angle of the sky above. I kept walking and I started feeling a tingle of hopefulness. The little voice inside me warned to brace myself for disappointment and a long, steep climb back up to the fence. The big voice inside me said, *Screw the little voice, we're going the right way, you're going to get home.*

Rebirth

After a bit, I came upon an enormous water tank and I knew I was on *somebody's* property now, but I didn't know whose. I kept walking and then I saw some trailers. *Are these the ones? Probably not, but could they be?* I kept walking. Then a beam of light hit my eye, blinding me for a fraction of a moment as a streak of sun emerged from behind a thick wall of clouds and landed right on that bright orange fireplace. That was when I knew, without a shadow of a doubt, that I wasn't lost anymore.

During my three and a half hours in the woods, Cerridwen followed me. She hunted me down as I ran in circles from myself until I crumbled to the ground and became that tiny grain for Her to consume. She birthed me into Her Wisdom and that is how I knew I could find my way. From that day forward, I would sing her praises.

And I knew the next time I was lost; I would meet Her again.

Shapeshifting Hen

Reti Toriella

A Blessing from Cerridwen

Molly Remer

Steep in the cauldron
at the crossroads,
that which has called you,
has beckoned you
to sink down and in.
Feel the bubbles collect
and the steam rise
and the flavors meld.
Marinate in your own life.
Let your layers sluice away,
become tender and soft,
hot and holy.
Say goodbye to could and should.
Liberate yourself
from obligation and expectation.
Rise steaming into the moonlight.
Accept your cloak of clarity.
Lay lapis beads around your neck.
Eat the pomegranate seeds.
Feel them tart against your tongue.
Feel the star shine
on your forehead
and the moon in your belly.
Take your next step.
The way is open before you
and you know where to go.

Prayer to Cerridwen

Rebekah Myers

Keeper of the Cauldron bright
Goddess, Seer, Mother, Crone,
Cerridwen, of dark and light
Grant us knowledge; mystic flight;
Resolute throughout the night,
Transformed, reborn, in your womb.

Green Goddess Giving Birth

Reti Toriella

Cerridwen Speaks

Janet Rudolph

I am multitude. I AM. I am undifferentiated potential carrying within my body all the gifts of manifest life and creativity. I am the dance of all potential. I am the inspiration and the agent that stirs these raw materials as the catalyst for creation, from the void to the manifest, from the unformed to the formed.

My first cauldron was the firmament, the bowl of the heavens from which I collected and gathered the treasures. I carried them to Earth in my own womb to fill the oceans, lakes, and rivers. In this way, my second cauldron became the Earth Herself, the womb of genesis. The words holy of holies come to mind although I prefer sacred of sacreds. I am known by other names including Tiamat, Saraswati, Ganga, Huixtocihuatl, and Oshun.

Waters are so key to life that we forget how violent their tempests can be. When I stir the Earth-cauldron, be forewarned! The storms I brew swirl with ferocity: Trees sway, structures come down, rivers flood. That's when people in their fear forget that this is the very same passion that propels creation. Your ancients knew this well. The Rig Veda called this primal basin of life *'unilluminated waters.'*[31] Genesis named it Tehom, the watery abyss of the deep. Homer referred to *"River Ocean, a deep and mighty flood, encircling land and sea... [as] the source of all."* [32]

I gathered elements from my first two cauldrons to create my third, the large metal kettle that is described in myths. Each cauldron may be smaller than the last yet each holds within, all of the same elements. My kettle that you know in myths hangs over flames

---

[31] Mircea Eliade, *From Primitives to Zen*, Harper and Row; 109.

[32] Charles Mills Gayley, *The Classic Myths in English Literature and in Art*, Blaisdell Publishing, reprinted, 1968; 3.

drawn upward from the Earth's core, the fiery heart at Her center. When it is still, not stirred or boiled, you can see the stars mirrored on its surface. But stir them and you will see that fiery vortexes of the heavens and the flowing earth eddies don't only reflect each other; they contain the very same essences.

Each drop of water you drink originated in the heavens, once sailed the seven seas, cycled through the packed ice of glaciers, mountainous waterfalls, rushing rainforest rivers and more. Each particle of water has gathered and compiled experience and knowledge from all corners of the world. My gift to you.

Oh, Gwion Bach when I engaged you to stir my cauldron, I knew you for your potential. If only you had understood, you would not have needed to run from me. When you splashed my sacred liquid of Star-Wisdom [33] onto your hand, brought it to your mouth, and ingested it, that was your own birthright knowledge. This was your dream and in manifesting its journey, it became the dream of all humanity. Your grand adventure was and is the same one that water takes, only in human form. You transformed into all manner of life to compile your own wisdom-experiences.

As your mythic story goes, you changed yourself into a rabbit, but I became a greyhound. You jumped into a river and became a fish, but I became an otter to continue the chase. You became a bird, but I became a hawk. And then, just as I was about to swoop, you jumped into the wheat pile and turned into a grain of seed. I became a hen, pecked through the pile, to find and eat you. In this manner I was able to retrieve and re-integrate this knowledge for myself.

As you yourself wrote, your adventures expanded beyond the myths. I can add to the tale of your exploits because I was there: You were the chick who pecked its own pathway out of its egg, a serpent rolling on the ground to shed its skin, a caterpillar who spun

---

[33] Eleanor Merry, *The Flaming Door*, New Knowledge Books, 148.

its own cocoon. You were the vibration of a newborn's cry, the conch as well as the wind that whistles through its corridors. You were the sap of the tree, the heart feather of a robin's breast, a thread on the loom of the fates, the mustard seed, the mighty oak.

You were all these and more. And as your journey came to fruition, we diverged our paths. This is the way of all life that comes to manifestation. Your journey opened pathways to enable me to share my secrets. And your own journey allowed you to grow into the wisdom-whisperer known as Taliesin of the beautiful voice. Proud mama that I am, I was the catalyst that pushed you to these teachings. In the end, I went back to my cauldron stirring. You continued to learn, decoding, and understanding the secrets of the stars. When you sang of the mysteries of life you created a pathway so that others could follow your lead.

One of those who followed you was a writer named Shakespeare. He understood how I energized my cauldron when he wrote, "Double, double toil and trouble," but alas he only focused on the chaos-producing effect of such stirring. I must admit, I do love that.

Shakespeare's witch's kettle was a mini version my own. Anywhere the waters are stirred is my domain. Here is my version of what Shakespeare's witches chanted.

> Triple triple, roil and ripple.
> Water's steam, fire's transmittal.
> Little by little, an enchanting tipple.

To those who hear my call, drink up and feel the revivifying liquids seep into your body and your spirit. I invite you each to take Gwion's journey to wisdom and selfhood and to become the Taliesin of your own life. In this, trust that I will always be there to give you swift kicks and challenges to propel you along your way. But also know this, I will also always be there to support you.

The Day Will Come

Sue Lobo

The day will come,
When men´s footprints will be washed away by women´s tears,
When women´s deep scars are removed, from walls of lost years,
When women´s backs will straighten, & their strength shall return,
When teardrops of all women, shall upon men´s consciences burn.

The day will come,
When all women down arms & say aloud, "Now you all go to hell,"
When women stir their cauldrons, & each cast their very own spell,
When women will know in their hearts, that there´s no need for fear,
When teardrops of all women, become their balm, & healing elixir.

The day will come,
When women´s smiles reach their eyes, & their laughter is heard,
When women stretch their broken wings, & fly off with free birds,
When women´s legs start walking tall, & through freedom´s door,
When teardrops of women stop, with words of "I´ll take no more."

The day will come,
When women raise up their arms, & hold tight each other's hands,
When women embrace one another, regardless of color & lands,
When women are united together, step strong, & all start to run,
When teardrops of all women dry, then their time´s finally come.

To Seek Ceridwen

Jhenah Telyndru

To seek Ceridwen is to seek our own breaking — our own unmaking... the dissolution of the self. It is to pursue a course of inner distillation... a catabolism into katabasis — a breaking down into our inherent elements so that we may become rarified in her alembic — so that we may be born anew from her cauldron.

To seek Ceridwen is to trade innocence for illumination, to trade limitation for liminality. It is to discover the furthermost edges of our being and the ways in which we must learn to step into the spaces of separation between ourselves and others — shapeshifting into new forms, new thoughts born of empathy, new perspectives arising from outmoded beliefs.

To seek Ceridwen is to see the truth of who we are in the waters of her cauldron. The light and the shadow, the fairness and the foulness. For we are Morfran and Creirwy both... part actualized, part hidden — part Sovereign, part Shadow... but the whole of us beloved by our Mother.

To seek Ceridwen is to pursue change — change of form, change of heart, change of mind. Hare into salmon, into wren, into seed. Into death and rebirth. Gwion into Taliesin. From small innocent into shining brow. And when the transformation is complete, she asks that we be an agent of change... shifting into that which she requires of us.

For she bids us sing with sharpest tongue that scolds and scalds the faces of tyrants with words forged in bile's righteous brew. And then, she asks for the balm of blessings dripping mead-sweet from our lips to soothe the mind and mend the hearts of those who are tested, those made weary by the trials of life... Until she asks for verses that conjure courage — that awaken sleeping souls into action, that embolden tentative whisperings into resounding shouts against injustice.

For once we get a glimpse, no matter how fleeting, of the world as it could be when banished is the darkness of deceit and avoidable death, of profit over people, of separation over community… for once our brows are set alight by her divine breath — our world will never be the same.

For…

> Our words are spells made manifest —
> Our poems, weavers of prophecy.
> Our songs reverberate in the darkness,
> catalyzing change and kindling light.
>
> > For it is through us that Ceridwen
> > Sings all things into existence
> > From whose cauldron streams the light of the Awen
> > From whose lips the songs of bards spill forth.
> > She who is the vessel of alchemical mystery
> > Through whose gates life surrenders
> > Through whose gates life is reborn.
> >
> > So let us sing of Holy Ceridwen
> > The bent, crooked woman
> > Who is the Sifter, and who is the Song…

Green Woman: Goddess of Wild Plants and Trees

Reti Toriella

In Praise of Cerridwen

Emma Clark

To be whispered over the vapours of a simmering pot
or over a crackling fire

You are the silence,
And stillness at dusk,
In the cauldron's heart,
Your dark bright light is found.

Lady of the woods,
Gatherer of spell songs,
Forager of phrase,
Collected by the wind.

Goddess of Wisdom,
Mystery weaver,
Nature's shapeshifter,
Walking through Annwfn's veil.

Old Sow of the land,
Protecting your young,
Milk, dew and acorns,
My offerings to you.

Mother of the tribe,
Beloved of Bards,
The Awen flows on,
And the songs will be sung.

Hound's paws like lightning,
Speeding over earth,
The magic is born,
From the elusive witch.

Otter in water,
The river runs fast,
Beauty in motion,
Quenching my thirst for you.

Hawk's eye at daybreak,
Circling earth, sea, and sky,
Queen of Lake Bala,
Your realm stretches beyond.

Black Hen pecks away,
The seed from the chaff,
I give myself up,
To transform in your womb.

****

You are the heart of my story,
You are the soul of my song,
With you at my side,
I can never go wrong.

The pot comes to the boil, and the embers of the fire glow with heat as the whispered words enter the world through my breath.

The Transformation of Her Cosmic Brew

Trista Hendren

"Witches cast spells, not to do evil, but to promote changes of
consciousness. Witches cast spells as acts of redefinition.
To respell the world means to redefine the root of our being.
It means to redefine us and therefore change us by returning us to
our original consciousness of magical-evolutionary processes.
This consciousness is within us, in our biology and in our dreams.
It works on subliminal levels, whether or not we are aware of it,
because it is the energy of life and imagination. When we are
aware of it, it works for us, as the energy of destiny. And it is
powerful, with the genuine power of biological life and
cosmic imagination." [34]

-Monica Sjöö and Barbara Mor, *The Great Cosmic Mother*

What could be more important during these violent and turbulent times than to reclaim our ancient herbal remedies and sacred spells? How do we take back our power? How to we bring the healing power of the Goddess into a world saturated with patriarchal thought?

Cerridwen is the Goddess of radical rebirth, transformation, and inspiration. Robin Wall Kimmerer wrote:

> "Action on behalf of life transforms. Because the relationship between self and the world is reciprocal, it is not a question of first getting enlightened or saved and then acting. As we work to heal the earth, the earth heals us." [35]

---

[34] Sjöö, Monica and Mor, Barbara. *The Great Cosmic Mother: Rediscovering the Religion of the Earth.* HarperOne; 2nd edition, 1987.

[35] Kimmerer, Robin Wall. *Braiding Sweetgrass: Indigenous Wisdom, Scientific Knowledge, and the Teachings of Plants.* Milkweed Editions; August 11, 2015.

Cerridwen's potion had to be boiled for a year and a day. Despite Her careful planning, the spell did not pan out as She had hoped. The takeaway for me is that not everything we ask for is meant for us—specifically when we ask for other people. While we all want the best for our children, they have their own lives to live—their own dreams and aspirations.

Cerridwen's love for her son is an invitation for us to radically love all the children of the world. We owe these little ones the same protection we would provide our own.

Yesterday I saw a video of children blown into the air. One child was torn in half. The other was blasted onto the top of a building where no one could safely reach him. I don't know at the time of writing this what happened to that boy.[36] I will never forget his small, bloodied face; his hand waiving for help as he cried out in pain. If he is alive, he surely will never forget this day for the rest of his life.

My best friend and I cried a long while together this morning having both seen this video. *How does a genocide continue in plain sight for over a year and a half?*

I always wait to write my piece until the very last minute. I often feel like these anthologies are so complete, there isn't really anything left for me to say. I found myself asking *what does it matter?*

Why does this work matter when there are children dying by the thousands?

---

[36] According to Palestinian journalist Samira Mohyeddin on Instagram at the time of publication, "Ali Faraj is the young boy. His father is dead behind him and his 5 sisters were also killed. One of them is severed in half on the wall to the left." His mother, Noha Mahmoud Shehto was wounded but also survived. 22 family members were killed. Most of them were children; siblings and cousins of little Ali.

People who love the Goddess don't kill children. Matriarchal societies do not destroy that which they create.

We need Goddess narratives more than ever. We need a massive change in consciousness. A complete overhaul. Patriarchy has to go. The love of the Great Mother will pull us through and push us forward.

These days, it is easy to be angry—enraged even. There are many things we have very little control over. But we have more power than we imagine. As Valarie Kaur wrote:

> "The opposite of love is not rage. The opposite of love is indifference. Love engages all our emotions: Joy is the gift of love. Grief is the price of love. Anger is the force that protects that which is loved. We cannot access the depth of loving ourselves or others without our rage." [37]

Cerridwen's story is relatable. *Who has not been consumed with rage after something cherished has been stolen?* As women, we have been violently disconnected from the inner wisdom of our own bodies—our blood, our pleasure, our milk. Patriarchy has cut off our bond with the Great Mother and to our connection with Mother Earth. It has severed the bonds to our children, to our own mothers, to our potential for joy... the list is endless.

When I feel discouraged, it is the plants and the animals who comfort me. I can spend just a few minutes in the dirt and feel better; tasting the herbs I have planted nourishes me. My dog and cat instinctively know when I need a cuddle. Feeding the birds is one of my greatest joys. I often imagine what it would be like to be in their animal body. *What would it feel like to sleep most of the day and let my body take a deep rest? What would it mean to fly?*

---

[37] Kaur, Valarie. *See No Stranger: A Memoir and Manifesto of Revolutionary Love*. One World; 2021.

We go through many transformations in our lifetimes. They are perhaps not as radical as shapeshifting into a greyhound, an otter, a hawk, or a hen. But we each have the capacity to become our Divine potential. As Barbara G. Walker wrote:

> "To each living thing the Mother gave a temporary form that would eventually dissolve, back once more into the infinite churning a cauldron of potential, where matters and energies are constantly exchanged and recombined. She made the world an image of that uterine cauldron, so that every life form sustains itself by absorbing, decomposing, and assimilating other forms." [38]

The shedding skin of the snake so prevalent in Goddess mythology has always been appealing to me as someone who has shapeshifted many times. Cerridwen's lore takes it a step further. Looking back at my own life, I am certainly not the submissive Christian daughter I was groomed to be. I had to acclimate through many drastic changes—truth seeker, feminist, Muslim, businesswoman, mother—before discovering what fit. And, I had to shed a lot that no longer did.

We must rid ourselves of the savior narratives many of us grew up with. The big father god is not coming to help. He often makes things worse with his writings of death and destruction. [39] Goddess Thealogy is a doctrine of action. She requires us to do the work.

In one of my favorite passages, Carol P. Christ summarized what I believe the heart of Goddess Spirituality is:

> "She changes everything She touches and everything She touches changes. The world is Her body. The world is in Her

---

[38] Walker, Barbara G. *Restoring the Goddess: Equal Rites for Modern Women*. Prometheus; March 1, 2000.

[39] See *Texts of Terror: Literary-Feminist Readings of Biblical Narratives* by Phyllis Trible, published in 1982, recently updated in a 40th edition.

> and She is in the world. She surrounds us like the air we breathe. She is as close to us as our own breath. She is energy, movement, life, and change. She is the ground of freedom, creativity, sympathy, understanding, and love. In Her we live, and move, and co-create our being. She is always there for each and every one of us, particles of atoms, cells, animals, and human animals. We are precious in Her sight. She understands and remembers us with unending sympathy. She inspires us to live creatively, joyfully, and in harmony with others in the web of life. Yet choice is ours. The world that is Her body is co-created. The choices of every individual particle of an atom, every individual cell, every individual animal, every individual human animal play a part. The adventure of life on planet earth and in the universe as a whole will be enhanced or diminished by the choices we make. She hears the cries of the world, sharing our sorrows with infinite compassion. In a still, small voice, She whispers the desire of Her heart: Life is meant to be enjoyed. She sets before us life and death. We can choose life. Change is. Touch is. Everything we touch can change." [40]

Let us choose life. Let us recognize that change is possible in this broken world we inhabit. It must and it will, whether for better or worse. I vote for better.

We have been stripped of our Divine nature for thousands of years. It is time to reclaim the Cauldron of Awen and re-story the world.

---

[40] Christ, Carol P. *She Who Changes: Re-imagining the Divine in the World*. Palgrave Macmillan; 2004.

List of Contributors

Alison Newvine is psychotherapist, writer and singer/songwriter living on Ohlone land in the San Francisco Bay Area, California. Her psychotherapy and coaching practice centers around trauma healing, spiritual inquiry, psychedelic integration/harm reduction, and empowerment work with women, gender expansive folks, couples and the queer community. Her writing is featured in *Pain Perspectives: Finding Meaning in the Fire*, and *Wounded Feminine: Grieving with Goddess* published by Girl God Books, as well as Mago Books' *Celebrating Intercosmic Kinship of the Goddess* and the upcoming anthology *Weaving Our Way Beyond Patriarchy* by Womancraft Publishing. She is also on the editorial board for Return to Mago e-magazine. Her band, Spiral Muse, produces original music dedicated to the Goddess and sacred feminist values and visions. You can learn more about her psychotherapy and coaching services at alisonnewvine.org and you can find the music of Spiral Muse at spiralmuse.band.

Andrea Redmond has been a feminist rights activist, artist and pagan for over 50 years. She has been a devotee of The Morrigan since she was a young girl.

She was born on Prince Edward Island, Canada of Irish descent and moved to Ireland with her young family and there, she was one of the first women in Belfast to paint wall murals. Her first mural in 1983 honoured women's rights activists from Ireland and South Africa. She has painted over 40 murals with similar themes and her work has been featured in a number of publications and films on Northern Ireland.

She has worked and chaired a number of women's, art and multicultural groups. She has taught programs in art, community development and youth work. She is a mother to three children and returned to education in her 40s, completing her PhD, at the University of Ulster.

Andrea currently resides in rural Donegal, Ireland where she operates her art studio / workshop. Her artwork is in permanent collections and galleries in Ireland, Canada and the United States.

Arlene Bailey is a visionary artist and author on the quest of "woman know thyself". Working in the realm of the Sacred Wild Woman in all her many visages, her paintings, poetry and prose reflect the raw, visceral and innate wild in all women, while also challenging and questioning everything we know to be true about the who of who we are as women walking in this time.

Through her magical weavings in word and paint and, drawing on her trainings and skills as an Ordained Priestess, Women's Mysteries Facilitator, Wise Woman Herbalist, Energy Medicine Practitioner and Retired Anthropologist, Arlene invites women to step into personal sovereignty as they listen to their ancient memories and voice of their soul.

Along with her three cats, this Wild Crone lives in North Carolina, USA. Currently, she is working on a book of her own art, poetry and prose.

Find her work below...

www.hersacredwild.com

www.facebook.com/hersacredwild/

www.thegirlgod.com

www.magobooks.com

Arna Baartz is a painter, writer/poet, martial artist, educator and mother to eight fantastic children. She has been expressing herself creatively for more than 50 years and finds it to be her favourite way of exploring her inner being enough to evolve positively in an externally-focused world. Arna's artistic and literary expression is her creative perspective of the stories she observes playing out around her. Claims to fame: Arna has been selected for major art prizes and won a number of awards, published many books, and—(her favourite) was being used as a 'paintbrush' at the age of two by well-known Australian artist John Olsen. Arna lives and works from her bush studio in the Northern Rivers, NSW Australia. Her website is www.artofkundalini.com.

Betsy Long grew up in Rome NY, and is now living in Socorro, New Mexico. She has lived all over the Rocky Mountains in the last 30 years. She recently married her high school love after being divorced from an 18-year marriage that wasn't right for her.

She is a self-taught artist, with 4 children (2 of her, 2 from her husband), and 3 grandchildren, one of which she is planning a Red Tent ritual for soon.

C. Ara Campbell is the author of *Dark Goddess Magick*, and founder of The Goddess Circle. She's a soul-guide, facilitator of *The Inner Priestess Awakening Online Journey and Relationship Empowerment & Sacred Love Online Journey*, and author of *The Astro Forecast* Publication. She is a contributing author on *Journeys with the Divine Feminine, Original Resistance: Reclaiming Lilith, Reclaiming Ourselves*, and contributing author and editor on *Kali Rising, Holy Rage.* Ara is a modern-day mystic dedicated to empowering others, connecting them with their purpose, living embodied truth and healing using the natural world. Ara is an old soul that has been writing and channelling cosmic guidance from the unseen since she was young, intuitively soul coaching using spiritual and natural energies. She can often be found seeking wisdom and solace in the wilds of Mother Earth, capturing the magic of nature with her camera, or snuggling her dog, Buddy.

Carolyn Lee Boyd's essays, short stories, memoirs, and poetry have been published in print magazines, internet sites, and book anthologies for over 40 years. Her novel, *The Temple of the Subway Goddess,* is about an ancient Goddess priestess miraculously transported to a distressed urban American neighborhood in the 1980s.

Her current writing explores goddess-centered spirituality in everyday life and how we can all better live in local and global community. She is currently writing a book on what ancient and contemporary cultures have to tell us about living in community today as well as a new novel. She lives in New England where she tends her tiny pollinator patch in the midst of suburbia and is amazed at the beauty of the cosmos in all its forms. Please visit her at her website, www.goddessinateapot.com, where you can find her writings and some free e-books to download.

Chelsea Arrington is a writer and poet. Her work can be found in the anthologies *Goddess: When She Rules, A Walk in a Darker Wood, Witch Lit: Words from the Cauldron*, the magazines, *Eternal Haunted Summer, Spectral Realms, The Audient Void, Weird Fiction Quarterly*, and *elsewhere*. She lives with her husband and their three children in the Greater Los Angeles Area where she hoards books and art and practices witchcraft with her coven sisters.

Claire Dorey

Editor: *Wounded Feminine: Grieving with Goddess*, Girl God Books. She is a regular contributor at Girl God Books, Return to Mago E-Magazine, and has been published in *She Summons: Why Goddess Feminism, Activism and Spirituality,* 2021, and *Celebrating Intercosmic Kinship of the Goddess*, 2023, both Mago Books. She illustrates her written work.

Her initiation upon the Goddess path occurred via ceremonial blessings by Priestesses in India. She is currently researching and intuitively interpreting meaning in ancient symbols from a feminist and cosmic perspective, using observation skills from her artistic training and by accessing creative wisdom from studying various healing practices, to try to see what ancient artists saw and feel how they felt.

Goldsmiths: BA Honors, Fine Art. Main Employment: Journalist and Creative, UK and overseas. Artist: Most notable group show, *Pillow Talk at the Tate Modern*. Included in the *Pillow Talk Book*. Curator:

3 x grass roots SLWA exhibitions and educational events focusing on Female Empowerment: Violence, Healing and Self. Current Artistic practice derives from the meditative, which she calls sending post-cards from the dark subconscious. She runs two 'closed' FB groups, *Esoteric Hissstories* and *Sirens at Source*. Teaching Workshops: Sculpture and Drawing. Extra study: Suppressed Female History and Goddess studies; Accessing Creative Wisdom; Sound and Breath Work; Reiki Master; Colour Therapy; Hand Mudras; Reflexology type massage; Sculpture.

Dorothy Collin is a mother, poet, animal rights activist and impassioned, though recent, believer in the message of the Goddess and its transformative power to create a new, kinder and much more sustainable world. Her first poetry collection is *One Hundred Days and Counting – Poems for Gaza* and her second entitled *Three Hundred Days and Counting* will be out soon. She is also writing a book about animal rights, the last great and unrecognised oppression. She can be found on Substack.com at 'Collapsing Upwards into Hope' as she works out the myriad of connections we all desperately need to discover on our journey to a brighter dawn for everyone.

Elizabeth SolArt is a solo artists creating a body of work called "Goddesses walking the Earth" where she is painting real women from the Spiritual, Pagan and Goddess Community as Goddesses! Her Mission is for women to see themself as the Feminine Divine; to see Goddess in the faces of their peers, friends, sisters, post lady, shop worker, artist, next door neighbour, family members, children grandmothers.. the list goes on...

Elizabeth SolArt works Intuitively with her pieces as a Priestess of Andraste and as a High Priestess of The Norpfolca Fenn, many Initiations on her path have culminated to her sole focus in art and connecting Deeply with the land in East Anglia.
Her body of work can be found on her FB platform:
https://www.facebook.com/share/1AKMMQvdop/

Emma Clark holds a PhD and teaches in the Department of Celtic and Scottish Studies at the University of Edinburgh. She has written books and articles on Celtic literature and has edited anthologies of Gaelic and Scottish poetry. The myth and symbolism of the land informs much of her research and she has always loved the magic at the heart of Celtic storytelling. Her first children's book was *Cerridwen and the Cauldron: a Celtic Tale of Magic.*

Erika Lopp is an anthropologist, writer and photographer. She received Bachelor of Arts degrees in both anthropology and sociology. Later she completed a master's degree in education and counseling psychology. She currently works for a Cultural Resource Management Firm, where her love for history and religious/cultural studies bloom. Her passions include an avid love for the realm of magic including mythology, magical herbalism, moon lore and spell craft. Her creative soul has led her to a love of gardening, art/crafts and baking. Things that inspire Erika: An open moonflower at dusk, the sunrise on a cool fall morning, and the distant call of the crow.

Esther Marcella Hoffmann is author of poetry collections, *Love Note To Gaia*, *Goddess of the Compass*, *Forest Breath*, and card deck, *The Doll Head Oracle a Journey Into Emotions*. A lifelong student of Archetypes, with a love of the Fool's Journey, she is a reader at E-Star Tarot. She lives in Minnesota, USA, and enjoys being among trees in the Northwoods and Lake Superior on the Northshore. Contact her at: estmarhoff@gmail.com

H. Byron Ballard, BA, MFA, is a native of Western NC. She is a writer, amateur folklorist with a specialty in Appalachian folk magic and healing. She tours extensively in the US and Great Britain. Her books include four on mountain folk magic. The first was *Staubs and Ditchwater*, and the most recent (2025) is *A Feral Church*. She lives in Asheville, NC. USA.

Hayley Arrington is a poet and mythologist. Her writings have appeared in various locations, including past Girl God publications *The Crone Initiation*, *In Defiance of Oppression*, *On the Wings of Isis*, and *Inanna's Ascent*. Recent writings can be found at *Eternal Haunted Summer*, *Alchemy of Miracles*, and SageWoman magazine (issues 84 & 96). In 2012, she received her MA in women's spirituality from the Institute of Transpersonal Psychology, where she wrote her thesis on sun Goddesses. She believes that myth is a verdant landscape where we can feel the Goddesses of old in the present. She is a devotee of Pelasgian Hera, Nebet-Het, and Brigid. Hayley is from the greater Los Angeles area, where she lives her sun-drenched days with her husband and son. Visit Hayley at https://loathlylady.wordpress.com/

Isaana B. Chrispin, daughter of Girl God author Sarah K. Grundy (Kelly Murphy), is an aspiring writer who finds inspiration in nature, poetry, and the complexities of human relationships. Her work often blends personal journeys with raw emotions, as seen in her poem Brewing the Moon Child, which delves into the dual nature of love—how it can both nurture and consume. For Isaana, poetry is like alchemy, transforming emotions into words and exploring the nature of the human heart. When she's not writing, she enjoys beach days, experimenting with new recipes, and getting lost in a good book. Through her stories and poems, Isaana invites readers to connect and share the journey.

Janet Rudolph is a wife, lover, mother, grandmother, seeker, finder, earth-breather, water-swimmer, there is no end to her descriptions. She has traveled to many sacred places in the world to soak up knowledge and experience culture. Along the way she earned two shamanic initiations and written a few books including *When Moses Was a Shaman, When Eve Was a Goddess,* and her recent autobiography, *Desperately Seeking Persephone.* In *Persephone*, subtitled, *The True Story of My Shamanic Journey Through the Underworld,* Rudolph describes her own personal quest which brought her from trauma through healing to joy. She also describes in vivid detail what shamanic initiations feel like.

Rudolph writes wherever and whenever she can to express, heal, inform, challenge, startle and to expand love. She is a contributor and co-weaver at /feminismandreligion.com/ You can also find her work at /mysticpagan.com/

Jeanine Otte (she/they) is the owner of JEO Speaks LLC and founder of the project, Our Nature is Our Way, reconnecting survivors of gender based violence with restorative practices for Self and Nature. Jeanine is a poet, writer, speaker, and social changemaker. Her life's mission is to inspire a radical shift toward a caring and reconnected world in which all life thrives. Jeanine is a certified conversation leader for a caring economy through the Center for Partnership Systems and a member of the Community Advisory Council with the Chicago Children's Advocacy Center. She is a survivor leader in the Sex Ed Works Coalition with the nonprofit Healing to Action. They have twenty years of professional experience developing programs, partnerships, and policy changes across government, nonprofit, and the energy/sustainability sectors. Jeanine's poetry has been featured in anthologies published by Girl God Books and performed at events. Jeanine is a partner to Carlos Ginard and parent to Malcolm, Michelle, and Nicole.

Jhenah Telyndru (MA, Celtic Studies) is a priestess, author, and educator. She founded the Sisterhood of Avalon in 1995, and serves as Academic Dean of the Avalonian Thealogical Seminary. A formally trained Celticist through the University of Wales Trinity Saint David, she also holds a BA (Hons.) in Archaeology from Stony Brook University. Jhenah hosts residential training retreats around North America and the UK, presents internationally at conferences and festivals, teaches online workshops and immersion programs, and facilitates pilgrimages to sacred sites in the British Isles through Mythic Seeker Tours.

Her published works include *Avalon Within: A Sacred Journey of Myth, Mystery, and Inner Wisdom* (Llewellyn, 2010), *The Avalonian Oracle: Spiritual Wisdom from the Holy Isle* (Schiffer Books, 2016),

Pagan Portals – Rhiannon: Divine Queen of the Celtic Britons (Moon Books, 2018), *The Mythic Moons of Avalon: Lunar and Herbal Wisdom from the Isle of Healing* (Llewellyn, 2019), *Pagan Portals – Blodeuwedd: Welsh Goddess of Seasonal Sovereignty* (Moon Books, 2021) and *The Ninefold Way of Avalon: Walking the Path of the Priestess* (Llewellyn, 2023).

As a member of clergy, Jhenah performs rites of passage in her community, and is in service as a Transpersonal Tarot Counselor and teacher. She is an Awenydd and Druid member of the Anglesey Druid Order (ADO), and is a certified Amicus Mortis (Friend of Death) through the Order. A priestess in the Avalonian Tradition for over 35 years, Jhenah has been following a Pagan path since 1986. To find out more about her and her work, she invites you to visit www.ynysafallon.com, https://linktr.ee/YnysAfallon
and www.sisterhoodofavalon.org.

Julia Jeffrey is a Scottish artist and illustrator. She studied painting at The Glasgow School of Art. Her faery and fantasy-themed work, of recent years, has attracted considerable acclaim and attention, with features in numerous international fantasy magazines. Her work appears on and in many books and albums, and her first tarot deck, *The Tarot of the Hidden Realm*, was published in 2013.

Kandice Mallinger, holds a B.A. in Women's Studies in Early Modern Europe with a minor in Islamic Studies. She is a certified Trauma Informed Yoga and Mindfulness Instructor. Kandice currently works for an internationally recognized treatment program that is an alternative to incarceration for women. She is a Peer Recovery Coach and Case Manager and enjoys a wide array of opportunities to work with women who are on a journey to change their lives. Kandice coaches clients on an individual basis; as well as facilitates groups including addiction and recovery, mindfulness, yoga, health and wellness and women's rights and empowerment which are integral to successful long-term recovery outcomes. Kandice initiated the trauma-informed Yoga Program that has become part of the required curriculum as well. Kandice is a passionate advocate for equity for women and girls, for reproductive rights, body sovereignty and other social justice issues. She is an outspoken, passionate and unapologetic feminist. Kandice facilitates in the public and private space offering yoga, mindfulness, yoga nidra and other practices focused on the Divine Feminine; as well as women's health and wellness.

Kat Shaw prides herself on breaking through the stereotypical views of beauty that have been cast upon society by the media, having made her name painting the glorious reality that is a woman's body.

Her nude studies of real women garnered unprecedented popularity within only a few short months, as women were crying out for themselves to be portrayed in art, rather than the airbrushed images of the perfection of the female form that are so rife in today's culture.

After graduating with a fine art degree, Kat achieved a successful full-time teaching career for 14 years, and continues to teach art part-time whilst passionately pursuing her mission of world domination by empowering as many women as possible to reach their fullest potential by embracing their bodies and loving themselves wholeheartedly.

Kat spreads her inspirational magic through her artwork, her Wellbeing business "Fabulously Imperfect", and her dedication to Goddess energy.

Reiki is a huge part of her life, and as a Reiki Master, Kat is committed to sharing Reiki, teaching Usui, Angelic and Karuna Reiki, and channelling Reiki energy through her artwork to uplift and heal.

As a Sister of Avalon, Kat also works directly with her Goddess consciousness, connecting to Goddess and Priestess energy and translating it into Divine Feminine infused paintings to inspire women and spread Goddess love.

Kat is also mum to a gorgeous teenage daughter, a bellydancer and an avid pioneer to improve the lives of rescue animals.

Kate Greenwood (7th December 1972 – 23rd December 2024) was a mother, a Priestess of Cerridwen, and a Witch with an affinity for wild nature and all of its magic. Kate had a deep and abiding love for the realms of story, mythology, folklore and fairy tales and was guided and nourished by them every single day. She lived amidst the forest and ocean landscapes of the Pacific Northwest on North America's far western shores where she and her family were in reciprocal relationship with the forestland that they dwelled upon.

Katie Daly is 10 years old and lives in Ireland with her artist mother Sannie Cuddihy, her D.J., dad Paul, Winston Dog, Casper cat and her hamster Peanut. Katie is a published writer and artist having contributed to Barbara O Meara's projects 'Home Words Bound' zine and 'Sort our Smears' community art campaign in 2019. Katie is inspired by nature and all things magical and mystical, loves music, dancing and cartwheels.

Kay Louise Aldred is a researcher, writer, and educator, who catalyses individual, institutional and collective evolution – through education, embodiment, and creativity – amalgamating metacognition, intuition, and instinct.

She has published three workbooks of her own with Girl God Books – *Mentorship of Goddess: Growing Sacred Womanhood, Making Love with the Divine: Sacred, Ecstatic, Erotic Experiences* and *Somatic Shamanism: Your Fleshy Knowing as the Tree of Life* – in addition to co-authoring *Embodied Education: Creating Safe Space for Learning Facilitating and Sharing* with her husband Dan Aldred. The couple reside in North Yorkshire, England.

www.kaylouisealdred.com
Instagram, Twitter and LinkedIn @kaylouisealdred

Kelly Murphy (Sarah K. Grundy) takes the name given to her at birth and of her maternal lineage for publications relating to her Celtic roots. She is the author of "Morgan," a soon-to-be-released story about the deep sea, lovers torn apart by tragedy, and the underwater world that serves as their only hope. "Morgan" translates as "sea-born," "sea-song," or "sea-circle" in the land of Kelly's origins. Her writing has been called "romantic," "life-changing," and "inspiring," and is published in the *New York Times*, political, women-empowerment films throughout Manhattan and California, clinical research for Ivy League Universities, The Girl God, as well for L'Oréal and Estée Lauder. Her Mazeylotus Goddess Project serves thousands of women globally with a mineral-based protocol and body integration e-book series for the root, solar plexus, and sacral chakras. Her new series, "The Great Irish Witch," reached up to 10,000 souls.

Lisbeth Cheever-Gessaman is the artist and illustrator of "The Divine Feminine Oracle" and "The Spellcasting Oracle." She is a scholar of the Divine Feminine, and a visionary artist who merges magick and technology with traditional mediums to create new interpretations of myth and archetype. Through her work she explores shamanic, astrological and mythological constructs to interpret the liminal worlds of the Divine Feminine, incorporating art and talisman to create a third phenomenon, or magical reality.

In honor of the Great Mother, and as personal witness, she creates all work under the pseudonym "SheWhoIsArt."

Website: www.shewhoisart.com
Facebook: www.facebook.com/shewhoisart
Instagram: shewhois

Lyn Thurman is an author, priestess, and artist living in a small sea-side town in North Wales. Her work centres around creating tarot and oracle decks that inspire self-discovery and spiritual growth. With a deep connection to the divine feminine, Lyn empowers spiritual entrepreneurs to tap into their intuition and bring their visions to life. Her creations are designed to help others navigate their personal and professional journeys with clarity and confidence, blending spiritual wisdom with practical guidance. In her new Welsh home, surrounded by nature's beauty, Lyn continues to explore themes of magic, creativity, and personal growth. You can find her at www.lynthurman.com

Maria Kefalogianni is of Cretan descent and lives in Manchester for over 17 years with her three kids and Irish husband. She is an emerging creatrix and mystic poet as well as a published writer in the studies of consciousness. By background, she is a university lecturer in counselling and psychotherapy for the past 12 years and a psychotherapist for over 16 years. She is also a supervisor for counsellors and holistic coaches and a sound healing practitioner with the voice and spiritual mentor . Her purpose in life is to be a bridge maker and a paradigm shifter. As a Neurodivergent creatrix she has birthed various communities. Above all, she is a lover of the liminal space in our daily lives and supports people to discover their sacred purpose and inherent wholeness. You can connect with her on digital platforms via her website:
https://www.presencecenteredpsychotherapy.com/

Molly Remer, MSW, D.Min, is a priestess, mystic, and poet in central Missouri. Molly and her husband Mark co-create *Story Goddesses* at *Brigid's Grove*. Molly is the author of many books, including *Walking with Persephone, Whole and Holy, Womanrunes, the Goddess Devotional, and* 365 Days of Goddess. She is the creatrix of the devotional experience *#30DaysofGoddess* and she loves savoring small magic and everyday enchantment.

Pat Daly (editor) is a mother of three daughters and proud grandma. A published author / writer on career and job search issues, Pat lives in Portland, Oregon.

Patricia Rose is a teacher, writer, and traveler. She is Hearing the Call to take part in the movement that will restore feminine mysticism and conscious sisterhood to its rightful place. Patricia has been on a slow lifelong journey of finding her voice, unwinding the harmful, psycho-spiritual conditioning left by patriarchal god-in-the-sky religion, and reclaiming the sacredness of the feminine. She is passionate about nurturing the inner knowing and wisdom that lies within and the powerful force that is sisterhood. To check out Patricia's news and offerings as she continues the journey, visit her website at www.sherose.org.

Pegi Eyers is a visual artist, independent curator and author of the award-winning *Ancient Spirit Rising: Reclaiming Your Roots & Restoring Earth Community*, a book that supports the recovery of authentic ancestral wisdom and traditions for all people. She self-identifies as a Celtic Animist and is a member of the Helena Clan (descended from "Mitochondrial Eve" as traced by The Seven Daughters of Eve), with more recent roots connecting her to the mythic arts of England and Scotland. Pegi lives in the countryside on the outskirts of Nogojiwanong in Michi Saagiig Nishnaabeg territory (Peterborough, Ontario, Canada), on a hilltop with views reaching for miles in all directions. www.stonecirclepress.com

Rebekah Myers is the founder/facilitator/curator of Sacred Sisters Full Moon Circle, which serves as a virtual Facebook and Instagram public page, a private Facebook group for women, and an actual women's circle that meets in-person.

Through these mediums, Rebekah seeks to amplify the voices and art of women, and to provide meaningful, enlightening ritual and celebration.

On International Women's Day in March of 2018, Rebekah was honored to have been one of five women recognized by KSL as Utah's most inspirational women.

Through her social anthropologist parents, Rebekah spent memorable time with the Iroquois (a matrilineal people) of Six Nations Reserve in Ontario, Canada. This experience significantly informed her life for the good.

Rebekah has had a life-long interest in and passion for folklore, mythology, and ancient history, and has spent significant time researching these worlds.

As a published writer, a teacher, director, award-winning singer/ actor, mother, and grandmother, Rebekah is devoted to edifying, educating, and empowering women.

Reti Toriella is a Cerridwen priestess from Estonia. Her passion is wildlife, trees and animals. She holds a deep connection with nature. Reti lives in the forest with her fox. She loves to express this magical beauty in her art and crafts. Reti knows how therapeutic painting and drawing is, like all creative activities. She gained this knowledge in art therapy at university. She loves music, deep shamanic drumbeats and Celtic lyrical tunes. Her son and daughter have given Reti three grandchildren, to whom she shares her grandmother's wisdom and love.

Rónán-Lukas Trodden is an emerging artist and author from Glasgow, Scotland. At 25, he has experience in both traditional and digital art and enjoys dabbling in the world of animation. He can be known to combine techniques from all three forms of art when it comes to creating his work.

Born and raised in a mixed-religion household, Rónán went wandering down the path of Paganism at an early age and never looked back, though it hasn't stopped him from being fascinated by various religions and faiths around the world. Despite being selective-mute, he speaks Scottish Gaelic and English and is relearning British Sign Language.

Dr. Sadie Laurenti Whitley is a heart-centered inspirational life coach, metaphysical ordained minister and holistic counselor, spiritualist and a shaman priestess that works mostly with women to find their joy after grief. As a life coach, she works with women who are ready to begin a new life to joyfully seek new opportunities after a divorce, the loss of a loved one, or the loss of a job. As a Reverend/Counselor, Priestess, and End of Life Doula, she assists in a heart-centered role to comfort those seeking a beacon of light within; inspiration and peace in their life with prayer, Reiki, blessings, rituals, and ceremonies. As a Priestess of Cerridwen in Avalon, she assists in healing modalities within the cauldron of Her loving heart. As a professional cook, she personally loves the metaphor of the cauldron brewing healing essences to bring you love and joy to your heart.

Sannie Cuddihy is an Irish visionary artist, Moon Mná Circle Facilitator, Medicine Spiral graduate, yoga teacher and Reiki practitioner living on the coast in Wicklow, Ireland.

Sannie's creative inspiration comes through sacred ritual, meditation, shamanic journeying and dream visions. She many exhibitions under her belt, both solo and group, including Abhainn Ri (2013-2015), 'Celtic Women in Art' with Barbara O Meara & Dee Mulrooney in 2022, VisionEire 2024, and 5 online exhibitions with the online art collective The Vision Train (2020-2024). Her installation piece Chrysalis was featured on Irish television show Super Garden (2022).

Her art and writing are also featured in the Girl God Book *Lady of the Forge*.

In 2023 Sannie was chosen as one of 18 international artists to travel to The Chapel of Sacred Mirrors, home of Alex and Allyson Grey, to study with world renowned visionary artist Amanda Sage.

Sannie combines all her trainings and knowledge to form a holistic practice which she applies to all her work and everyday life.

You can find her work at www.sannie.ie

https://www.instagram.com/sanniecuddihyart/

Sharon Smith is a writer, ghost writer, editor, and proofreader with a passion for helping women reconnect with their Authentic Selves and Voices. She loves and honors the Great Mother in all Her many forms and has a deep connection to Nature. She identifies as a

Green Witch and follows an eclectic spiritual path that is a blending of Native American and Celtic Teachings, both in her ancestral line.

Sue Lobo is the author of five books of her own and co-author with worldwide poets in another twenty-one publications. She has also participated in poetry competitions in Gibraltar and Spain. She is married to a Spaniard, with two grown up sons and two grandsons and presently lives in Spain. Her book of poetry about death and dying called "The Last Dance" was reviewed on Italian television and has been used to comfort the bereaved in hospices and also used at funerals. She champions women and their fight for equality around the world and especially the age of women's Cronedom. As a child she grew up in the Kalahari Desert in Botswana among the Bushmen who taught her the beauty and magic of nature and unity of the tribe. She was born in England and has lived in many countries which has influenced her work. Sue writes poetry daily and can be followed on Facebook.

Susan Morgaine is a Priestess, Traditional Herbalist, Writer, and Teacher.

She has taught Kundalini Yoga and Meditation for over 20 years, being a Certified instructor through the Kundalini Research Institute; additionally, she is certified in Chair Yoga. She is a Certified Women's Empowerment Coach. She has long been involved in Goddess Spirituality and Feminism, teaching classes and workshops, including Priestessing local Red Tents.

She is a former monthly columnist with PaganPages.org Her writings can also be found in The Girl God Anthologies, *Whatever Works: Feminists of Faith Speak* and *Jesus, Mohammed and the Goddess*, as well as Mago Publications *She Rises, Volume 2*, and *Celebrating Seasons of the Goddess.* She is the author of *My Name is Isis, the Egyptian Goddess*, part of the *My Name is* series of children's books. She has also been published in *Jareeda* and *SageWoman* magazines and has a book of poetry published. She is a Reiki Master, as well as a Crystal Specialist. She can be found at MysticalShores.com.

Terence Estrada is an embodied artist who captures the essence of the divine feminine through her artworks. Each piece acts as a portal to her dreams, intentions and visions which are then manifested into a sacred marking. An adornment of one's inner journey.

Terence has worked professionally as a tattoo artist since 2017. She also dedicates herself into learning new styles, art forms and to lead an overall creative lifestyle.

Terence also encapsulates her Filipino heritage through her highly influenced Kalinga designs. Tapping into her creative potency her style has further developed into larger ornamental pieces, all in which signifies healing, courage and empowerment.

Website: https://tradz.store/
Instagram: @t.radz

Trista Hendren founded Girl God Books in 2011 to support a necessary unravelling of the patriarchal world view of divinity. Her first book—*The Girl God,* a children's picture book—was a response to her own daughter's inability to see herself reflected in God. Since then, she has published more than 50 books by a dozen women from across the globe with help from her family and friends. She lives in Bergen, Norway. You can learn more about her projects at www.thegirlgod.com.

Trista's Acknowledgments

I would like to acknowledge my co-editors. My mother, **Pat Daly,** has edited all my books. There would be no Girl God Books without her enormous contributions. I was also thrilled to work with my dear sister **Emma Clark** on this project. Her cheerful voice brightened my day throughout this project.

Many thanks to the ever-inspiring **Byron Ballard** for writing the brilliant Preface.

Tänan teid, **Reti Toriella** for your beautiful cover art and illustrations throughout this book and the earlier children's book.

A special acknowledgement to **Jhenah Telyndru** for her in depth paper, "Ceridwen - Divine Muse and Mother of Awen." I knew you had something important to say, but you blew away my expectations.

Enormous appreciation to my husband **Anders Løberg**, who prepared the document for printing and helped with website updates. Your love, support and many contributions made this book possible.

Lastly, I would like to thank my dear sisters **Tamara Albanna, Glenys Livingstone, Dorothy Collin, Jessica Bahr, Susan Morgaine, Lisa Smith, Sharon Smith, Arlene Bailey, Kay Louise Aldred**, **Rebekah Myers, Arna Baartz, Kat Shaw,** and **Alyscia Cunningham** for always being right there to cheer me on in the spirit of true sisterhood.

Thank you to all our readers and Girl God supporters over the years. We love and appreciate you!

Emma's Acknowledgments

Thank you to my Cerridwen Kin from all over the world who have shared in ritual and ceremony together, online and in-person. Your inspiration and wisdom gives me so much joy!

Thank you to **Trista**, for this journey we have been on with Cerridwen, for your support, and for the kindness and generosity you have shown me in all that we've done together.

And thank you to **Peter**, for your endless love and support.

If you enjoyed this book, please consider writing a brief review on StoryGraph, Amazon and/or Goodreads.

Be sure to check out
Cerridwen and the Cauldron: a Celtic Tale of Magic
– a children's book by Emma Clark, illustrated by *Reti Toriella*

Upcoming Publications from Girl God Books

Asherah: Roots of the Mother Tree – Edited by Claire Dorey, Janet Rudolph, Pat Daly and Trista Hendren

Kali Ma: the Dark Mother – Edited by C. Ara Campbell, Jaclyn Cherie, Pat Daly, and Trista Hendren

Sacred Breasts: an Inspirational Anthology for Living Your Breast Life – Edited by Barbara O'Meara, Trista Hendren and Pat Daly

Lady of the Forge: Stories and Art Dedicated to the Goddess Brigid – Edited by Isca Johnson, Trista Hendren, and Pat Daly

Solstice Carols: Remembering the Great Goddess – *Edited by Trista Hendren, Sharon Smith and Pat Daly*

http://thegirlgod.com/publishing.php

Printed in Great Britain
by Amazon

61731839R00127